I0819047

PRAISE FOR *FIRST-TIME FOSTERING*

"*First-Time Fostering* is the practical, compassionate guide new foster parents have been longing for. Laura anticipates the questions, fears, and complexities of fostering and responds with trauma-conscious, evidence-based insights and tools that are both respectful and deeply attuned to children's needs. This book is clear, direct, and genuinely useful for anyone stepping into this vital role."

—Bryana Kappadakunnel, LMFT,
author of *Parent Yourself First*

"This book is an essential guide for new and potential foster parents! Laura the Foster Parent Partner paints a realistic picture of the foster parenting experience using carefully curated scenarios. Her direct and compassionate tone encourages readers to embrace this complex and meaningful role, especially during a time of intense rupture in a child's life. Learn how to use practical tools and self-awareness to navigate the unknowns with a sense of agency."

—Lauren Stauble, foster mama and bestselling
author of *Tiny Humans, Big Emotions*

"Laura's thoughtful considerations and questions for new foster parents honestly brought me to tears. Her reminders to consider the child's perspective show real intentionality. This book gives me hope that kids in foster care will have a better experience than I did. I wish my foster parent had understood trauma-informed, intentional parenting like this."

—Tina Bauer, former foster youth,
educator, and advocate

"Laura's heart, experience, and insight shine through in this guide—every page offers real-world tools and compassion for foster parents navigating the ups, downs, and in-between. This is an essential read for anyone stepping into fostering and committed to making a lasting positive difference in a child's life."

—Rob Scheer, founder of Comfort Cases,
former foster youth and father of five children
adopted from the foster care system

"As someone who grew up in foster care and has been a foster parent, I can tell you: This is the book I wish existed years ago. *First-Time Fostering* is the first guide I've seen that truly lays out the 'how to' of fostering with clarity, compassion, and hard-earned wisdom. It's practical in all the ways that matter—real scripts, real strategies, real stories—offered without judgment and grounded in what kids actually need. And just like the oxygen-mask rule on airplanes, this book helps caregivers take care of themselves so they can show up fully for the children they love. It's the CliffsNotes every foster and kinship parent deserves—honest, actionable, and a lifeline when moments get tough."

—David Ambroz, author of
A Place Called Home

"Laura leaves no stone unturned, revealing both the joy and strain of opening your home and heart to a young person in foster care. The book is approachable and full of wisdom and insights. It's like having a very knowledgeable best friend on speed dial. I wish I had this book before I began fostering."

—Mark Daley, social activist, entrepreneur,
foster turned adoptive father, and author of *Safe*

"*First-Time Fostering* fills a gap foster parents have felt for years. Laura's trauma-informed, inclusive guidance captures the realities, challenges, and hope of foster parenting while offering tools that truly make a difference. If you're thinking about fostering, are in the process of getting licensed, or are currently fostering and looking for support and encouragement, this book is for you."

—Brittany Burcham Collins, former foster parent, former court-appointed special advocate (CASA), and content creator

"*First-Time Fostering* is one of the most genuinely useful, inclusive, and honest books I've read on caring for children in foster care, grounded in 'trauma-conscious' practice that is respectful of children, parents, and those stepping in. You can read it cover to cover or jump straight to the chapter that meets you where you are in the journey, and the guidance still lands, offering the practical, nuanced details that foster parent training simply doesn't touch. The scripts for difficult conversations, paired with thoughtful resources, examples, and scenarios, feel like the kind of support you'd only get from a seasoned mentor and make this essential reading for anyone stepping into fostering. This is the book I would hand to anyone considering fostering and, frankly, to every current foster parent as well."

—Ali Caliendo, executive director of Foster Kinship

"By creating this comprehensive, practical guide to foster parenting, Laura has provided an invaluable service for caregivers supporting young people in the child welfare system. Every chapter resonated with my own experience as a foster parent. I highly encourage anyone thinking about fostering to read this book!"

—Matt Strieker, CEO of United
Friends of the Children

"This book balances empathy with actionable insight, providing the understanding and encouragement that make all the difference in navigating the foster care experience. I wish every new foster parent had this on day one. It offers clear guidance, compassion, and practical tools that every new foster parent deserves. It's a resource that will help families feel seen, supported, and more prepared as they navigate the foster care experience."

—Kristen Gingrich, LCSW, CADC, CCS

"Laura is a wayshower, giving foster parents a generous gift of information and encouragement with this robust guidebook. What shines through most, however, is Laura's heart for cultivating a stable, safe, and trauma-informed environment for every child while expertly coaching parents on how to best navigate home, school, and community situations. I foresee many dog-eared and underlined pages in every chapter!"

—Marianne Richmond, children's author,
MA Clinical Mental Health Counseling

"Laura the Foster Parent Partner's *First-Time Fostering* is a wise, loving, and deeply practical resource. I'll be recommending it to every foster parent I meet."

—Lisa Sibbett, creator of the Auntie Bulletin

"As someone who has navigated the child welfare system as a foster parent, I wish this book had existed when I started my journey. Laura provides the honest, actionable advice that training classes can't cover—from the first phone call to the daily realities of caring for kids who've experienced trauma. This is the manual foster parents actually need!"

—Jeanne Vallor, foster parent
and content creator

"With compassionate storytelling, easy-to-understand instruction, and relevant real-world examples, *First-Time Fostering* is a must-read for all foster parents, first-time or otherwise! In *First-Time Fostering*, Laura provides a framework for foster parents to support both themselves and the children in their care, using a trauma-conscious approach to address challenges with feeding, sleeping, bathroom needs, and more. From sample scripts to planning checklists, this is more than a guidebook—it's actionable support for the parents who need it most."

—Mallory Whitmore, M.Ed., founder of the
Formula Mom and author of *Bottle Service*

first-time fostering

A PRACTICAL GUIDE FOR SUPPORTING KIDS IN FOSTER CARE

LAURA the foster parent partner

Cover design by Lauren Michelle Smith
Cover images © Igor Levin/Shutterstock, Gemma can fly/Stocksy
Internal design by Laura Boren/Sourcebooks
Internal art by Lindsey Cleworth

Published by Sourcebooks
1935 Brookdale RD, Naperville, IL 60563-2773
(630) 961-3900
sourcebooks.com

Cataloging-in-Publication Data is on file with the Library of Congress.

Printed and bound in the United States of America.
VP 10 9 8 7 6 5 4 3 2 1

Contents

Let's have a quick chat.

Hi there, I'm Laura! I'm guessing you purchased this book because you don't have a lot of time (or energy!) and you need some ideas on how to work through a particular foster parent situation. Or perhaps you're interested in foster care and want to get a sense of what being a foster parent is really like. Either way, I've got you covered, and I will do my best to be direct and to the point.

I am a former foster parent, and I currently mentor and support new and hopeful foster parents as they work within the foster care system and care for kids in their home.

For the past several years, I've had the honor of creating an online space where millions of people have stopped by to share their ideas, tips, and tricks for day-to-day foster care situations. My audience consists of not just new and hopeful foster parents, but experienced caregivers, therapists, attorneys, foster care workers, educators, daycare providers, current and former foster youth, advocates, nonprofit volunteers, policymakers, and compassionate community members who want to show up for kids in foster care and their families.

I've spent the last four years reading through thousands of community comments and pulling together shared wisdom into this practical guide. The insights shared here are grounded in my personal experiences and training and enriched by the experiences of people impacted by and working within the system. Professionally, I've spent years in consumer research, gathering and summarizing qualitative insights through focus groups and interviews. It's been incredibly meaningful for me to apply this expertise here. This book is a compilation of my online work: I have synthesized and summarized advice into practical, bite-size insights to help you get started and feel confident in these new foster parenting moments.

You can use the table of contents to jump to what you need help with right now, or if you haven't started fostering yet, I recommend reading the chapters in order to get up to speed on what's to come so you feel prepared and confident. There is also a detailed glossary in the back if you get stumped on a specific term or acronym.

But okay, one last thing before you dive in: Please remember that these considerations and ideas are just a starting point. Every child is different. Every situation is different. Every worker and child welfare department are different. Not every tip will work for you. My hope is that something within these pages will spark new ideas for you or provide another strategy to try during one of the more difficult moments.

I want to align on some things before you dive in. This is important.

In this book, I talk in a direct way about topics that may be triggering.

For example, I share about considerations related to sexual, physical, or domestic abuse, self-harm and suicide, neglect, food insecurity, and beyond. Nothing I describe is graphic, but through creating content around these topics, I've found that some of them may surprise you and be upsetting in ways you might not anticipate. So because of that, I wanted to share this gentle warning as you dive in.

I also use language that may be different from what you are used to, including:

Foster parent—Any person who is caring for a child in foster care. Depending on where you live or your specific situation, you may be more familiar with other terms, like "resource parents," "caregivers," "kinship providers," "host family," or "care provider." In this book, "foster parent" is a stand-in for any and all of these groups.

Parent—The person who was parenting the child prior to the child entering foster care. This definition is specifically inclusive to cover a variety of parents including bio parents, relatives that had full custody, or an adoptive parent. This is the parent who is working toward reunification.

Permanent child—Any kid who is a permanent member of your family. This could be a biological child, adoptive child, or stepchild, or a child who is with you permanently through guardianship.

Worker—When I use this term, I'm referring to the case manager, caseworker, or social worker who is assigned to support the child and their family.

KEEP AN EYE OUT FOR THESE ICONS WHILE YOU READ:

An extra piece of information you may want to consider more closely.

A *starting point* for a script you can use. Modify this for the child, situation, and need. It is just a place to begin to help you feel confident in this moment.

✕ I use this when I'm giving you an example of what not to do or say. It's so you don't get confused when reading a list quickly.

Think of this book as a handheld support group. It is a collection of tips and considerations and a starting point for discussions. It is not professional advice.

This book is not offering professional advice (legal, medical, therapeutic, etc.), services, or treatments. Suggestions and ideas are crowdsourced and for informational use only. If there is ever a concern, it's important to speak to a professional about what's best for the child in your care. This could be the child's worker, therapist, teacher, doctor, attorney, or other professional in their life.

And lastly, I have a confession.

In writing this book, there were many nights where I lay in bed worrying that someone would pick up this book and decide that foster care would be too hard for them, and they wouldn't even try. But at the same time, if I am vague about the realities of the system and step over the details and nuances, that doesn't really help someone feel prepared and confident to begin and to say yes.

All that is to say, please understand that this compilation of experiences and foster care situations is *vast*. I am summarizing experiences and tips from thousands of comments and messages. You will not experience all of the things in this book. The kids you care for will not need *all* of this careful advice for every single moment of the day. I included all of these details in case something does come up. I hope to be there to support you so you can feel confident meeting needs and providing care.

Thank you for taking the time to consider fostering, and thank you for caring so much about supporting kids and families impacted by foster care.

Part 1

Laying the groundwork for a successful beginning—your future self will thank you!

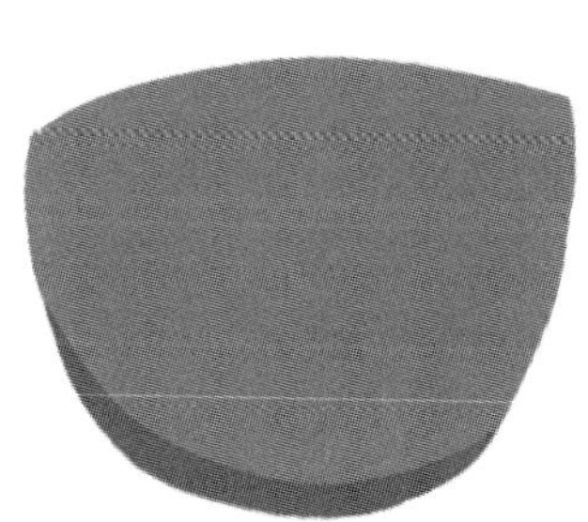

I signed up to open my home...

But it was my heart and mind that had to open first.

1

Becoming a Foster Parent

TL;DR: Get all the important info ahead of time at an introductory session. Ask any and all questions. Throughout the process, scan everything, stay organized, and explore as many training opportunities as possible.

Thank you for taking this step to learn more about becoming a foster parent. The fact that you've gone as far as reading a book on the subject speaks volumes and tells me you have a big heart and care deeply for your community. You are about to embark on a life-changing journey for you and your entire family. You'll be making a real, tangible impact on your community, and for that, I thank you.

The work you do before you say yes is very important and is often overlooked or rushed. Becoming a foster family is disruptive, and unprepared families may face personal challenges if they aren't set up and ready.

Questions to Ask Before You Begin

In the United States, foster families are typically licensed directly by the county or state they live in or through a private agency that is contracted by that county or state. Some places offer you the option to choose between getting licensed through an agency or the county, while other parts of the country only have one option for licensing.

Regardless of your options, it's important to get as much information up front as possible to avoid any possible issues down the road. I've compiled a ton of question topics for your consideration. Narrow this list down to what matters most to you. Ask these questions at an info session, orientation or when a worker visits your home for the first time at the beginning of the licensing process. Don't be afraid to speak up with your questions.

- Where and when do classes take place (virtual, in person, nights or weekends, etc.)?

If you are a relative who is concurrently providing care for the youth while getting licensed, ask about expedited training options available to kinship providers.

- When and where do CPR and first aid classes happen? How much do they cost?
- How long does it typically take people to get fully licensed from start to finish?
- Do you license single foster parents?

You may want to ask to speak with other single foster parents. You might get better day-to-day information from them directly.

- Is there a limit as to how many kids you will place in my home?
- Do you license specialized foster homes, like medical or therapeutic

foster homes? Or do you have any other limitations on what children your agency places (like age or case specifics)?

> Some agencies are strict about what children they will place. For example, if you are getting licensed to foster a possible relative or sibling, you should make sure that the agency will allow that.

- What fees/costs should I expect when getting licensed?

> There are costs in becoming a foster parent—it isn't free! These fees could include purchasing safety items for your home (like a pool fence), fronting the cost for the fingerprinting or scans for other adults in the home, first aid classes, co-pays for visiting your doctor to complete the health questionnaire, childcare expenses while you are getting trained, and beyond.

- Are you LGBTQ+ friendly?

> You may want to ask to speak with other LGBTQ+ families who are currently fostering. While some places may say on their website that they are welcoming or nondiscriminatory to LGBTQ+ families, they may not actually be inclusive in practice (for example, denying families from being licensed, not placing children in homes, or exclusionary events like "Foster Mom Brunch").

- Are you affiliated with a religion? How does that impact the day-to-day operations or expectations of foster families?
- Do you have an "adoption matching" or "waiting child" program?

(This would be relevant if your family is open to being a forever family for a child.)

> You may also want to ask how long families typically wait to be matched, or if there are specific classes you are required to take to be an adoptive home.

- Why should I choose your agency vs. others or vs. the county?
- What type of support do you provide for the children you place in a home (such as clothing reimbursements, in-house mental health professionals, youth support groups, daycare reimbursement, etc.)?
- What case services do you provide, such as monitoring parent visits, transportation support, etc.?
- Do you have someone I can call after hours or in case of an emergency?
- What hours during the week do workers typically conduct home visits?
- What are the requirements for babysitters or daycares I may use?
- Do you have respite providers for foster parents? How does that process work?
- Do you offer a foster care support group? If so, is childcare provided during those groups?

> Don't forget to search for reviews on Yelp or Google, and look for reviews posted by foster parents.

Steps to Getting Licensed to Foster

Once you've attended an orientation, completed your research, and determined how you will be licensed, your licensing worker should have things relatively laid out for you in terms of the steps to getting licensed. If that isn't the case, below are some general steps you can expect when you are getting licensed. The order may be different depending on your licensing worker and state or county policies. There may be added steps not listed here, especially for agencies that place kids with higher levels of care needs.

- **Complete paperwork.** This includes a formal application, financial records, health records, and references.
  - » Ask for a checklist of all the paperwork, so you can make sure you are being efficient. For example, if you need a form filled out by your doctor and a TB test, it may be most efficient to do that all in the same appointment.
  - » Scan *everything* you hand over, so you have a copy! Paperwork goes missing or workers change, so having copies on hand can be helpful. Take it a step further, and organize everything virtually in a folder system so that you can easily email or text documents to the licensing worker as they're needed.
  - » Make sure you let your references know ahead of time so they can be on the lookout through email or regular mail. Let them know they need to return the reference packet immediately.

- **Complete a background check.** This is usually required for all adults in the home, even adult children who will not be actively participating in foster parenting. Expect longer waiting periods if you have moved states in the past ten years.
  - » Ask if they have a service provider to do fingerprinting for free, or if they will reimburse for this service once you are licensed.
  - » Many places have waivers for relatives of the foster parents if

something comes up on a background check, depending on the nature of the offense, length of time since it has occurred, etc., as it is important for kids to be with family when safe and possible. You can seek legal counsel if there is a concern or would like to appeal.

- **Take classes.** This includes foster care preservice training classes, first aid, CPR, water safety, and beyond.
    - » If there is an opportunity to get specialized training for advanced care (like medical or treatment foster care), you may want to sign up for that training now before your life becomes very busy with foster parenting!

- **Complete a home study.** This is a comprehensive evaluation of your family that the agency or county will use to determine whether you are fit for fostering. There are often formal interviews with everyone in the home, as well as informal conversations and observations along the way. Note that some workers may want to interview the children in your home privately or speak with your adult children, former spouses, or others who are familiar with your parenting.
    - » You may be able to find a copy of the home study questions for your county online so you can see the types of things that will be discussed. You don't need to prepare responses to these questions ahead of time, but it may be helpful to think about some of the more sensitive topics, and how these things will influence how you foster and approach parenting.

- **Complete a home inspection**. This is a room-by-room walk-through of your home to ensure it is a safe environment that complies with all relevant state, county, and/or agency policies.

» Get the home inspection checklist at the beginning of licensing. There may be costly things you must do to your home to be compliant. For example, we had to replace some old windows that didn't function properly, which was very expensive!
» If you are a former foster youth or have experienced childhood trauma, you may want to mentally prepare to be asked about this. Having childhood trauma often does not disqualify you, but workers will likely ask how you worked through these experiences and the impact it has had on your life and parenting.

During your training, be sure you get as much information as possible in writing. This will vary depending on your county, but this can include a foster parent handbook, the Foster Parent and Foster Child Bill of Rights, foster parent policies or directives, etc. These documents may be *referenced* during training, but follow up and ask for a copy or link to where you can find them in full online. Be persistent, because if anything comes up in the future (such as a false allegation, rights being violated, etc.), you will want to make sure you have a clear understanding of protocols and procedures.

Go Deeper with Your Training

Your foster parenting preservice training will hopefully cover many topics, but it's unrealistic to think it will fully prepare you for the challenge of welcoming a child you do not know into your home. Use these resources to expand knowledge of foster care (in addition to this book!):

Social media: An easy way to hear about a variety of lived experiences is through social media. My work was born here, and I learn each and every day from the variety of creators across the child welfare community. You can follow former foster youth, current foster parents, adoptees, workers, family law attorneys, nonprofits, and beyond. Additionally, in many states and counties, you can find active Facebook groups or subreddits where foster parents gather, share resources, and get advice. Reading through the posts can give you a sense of what possible challenges may come up for you when navigating your local system.

Books by former foster youth: I encourage you to read books by former foster youth to get a more direct understanding of what it's like to live in the system. There are many authors and themes to explore. Find a few to read to ground yourself in the importance of child-centered parenting methods and advocacy within the system.

Inclusive caregiving: Kids and families you will support will come from all backgrounds, cultures, and beliefs. Consider exploring training topics like implicit bias, textured hair care, supporting LGBTQ+ youth, and parenting neurodivergent children.

Media: Further your knowledge by watching shows about foster care, such as *Foster* on HBO, the movies *We Gotta Get Out of Here* and *Closure*, the TV show *The Day I Picked My Parents*, and the series *ReMoved* on YouTube. Despite some of the far-fetched plotlines and soapy nature of the show, my husband, Chris, and I even enjoyed *The Fosters* (a fictional young adult TV drama), the original *Lilo & Stitch* movie (2002), and the movie *Luck*. You can also watch movies from the parents' perspective, like *I Am Sam* or *Take Care of Maya*. You can also find many podcasts about trauma-informed parenting and foster care.

News: Consider signing up for internet alerts (such as Google Alerts) for foster care–related news for your county or state. It will give you a good sense of what the key issues are in your area, and it will also keep you up-to-date on new initiatives, nonprofits, and policies.

Volunteer: While you are waiting for paperwork to be processed, you can step into the community by volunteering for local foster care organizations or community organizations that support families in crisis, such as food banks, shelters for unhoused families, or domestic abuse shelters. This personal, hands-on experience can help you start to understand the complexities of the system and family needs.

Share what you are reading, watching, and listening to with your friends and family who will be supporting you on your foster parenting journey so they can learn as well!

HEAR DIRECTLY FROM A FOSTER PARENT

"We read as much as we could about trauma and the way it impacts young brains, and we listened to former foster youth who had lived out this experience as often as we could. It helped us navigate things when our teenage placements seemed to react to things we thought were nonissues, and helped us avoid certain pitfalls because we had learned from others."

2

Aligning with Your Family and Community

TL;DR: Having honest, open conversations with everyone in the home and your friends and family is an important step in making sure everyone is on the same page. Everything from budgets, family traditions, permanent kids' needs, work, scheduling, and boundaries should be discussed.

Foster parenting will challenge you and your relationships in new ways. Aligning your family and support network early builds a strong foundation for fostering. Outlining predetermined boundaries, areas of flexibility, and nonnegotiables will be an important road map in your fostering journey.

In this chapter, I'll offer many considerations and conversation starters, but don't expect this topic to be one you can quickly check off your list. The reality is that these conversations unfold at their own pace and can't be figured out all in one sitting. You may need to come back to this chapter several times, and that's *a good thing*. You've been thinking about fostering for a while, but for your friends and family, this may all be brand-new. Giving them the opportunity to learn and engage with you about what fostering really means, why you want to do it, and why their support is important to you will help them feel valued and more invested in your journey. I promise these steps will be worth your time and energy.

Self-Reflections and Immediate Family Conversations

It's a good time to reflect.

You are about to embark upon a life-changing experience. Even if you are a relative and stepping in without much notice, it can be important to pause to make sure you consider all aspects of your life, so you are prepared. If you are a first-time parent, it's okay if you don't have all the answers.

Consider the following thought starters. For those parenting with a partner, have these conversations together.

General parenting:

- What are my strengths as a parent?
- What are my areas of need as a parent?
- What parenting task am I most looking forward to?
- What parenting task am I least looking forward to?

Foster parenting:

- What age, gender, and other specifics am I comfortable with when taking placement calls? What are my limits?

> For counties with intensive needs, you may get a call for placement while you are still getting licensed. It's good to have this conversation early, just in case this happens.

- What day of the week do I want to keep free from any foster care meetings?

Keeping one day a week or one week clear each month of foster care–related appointments can give everyone in the home a break. Of course, a child's visits with their parent(s) are court ordered and must happen per that schedule. These visits can be in person, on video, over the phone, or some combination of all three.

For couples:

- How will placement calls be handled? Who is taking the call? Do we need to talk to each other before saying yes? Under what circumstances can the point person say yes? Do we need to conference call the other person in? What should we do if one of us can't reach the other?
- Who will be using FMLA (Family and Medical Leave Act) benefits?
- Who will handle drop-off and pickup at school?
- How will we determine who supports the child at therapy, visits, etc.?
- Who will attend meetings?
- How will we divide up the foster care–related tasks?
- Who will be in charge of paperwork?
- Who is the primary contact for workers?
- Who will be the primary contact for parents?
- Who will manage the emails, or are we creating a shared email address to use?

Personal and family needs:

- How will I support my permanent children (if you have them)? What are the boundaries or rules when it comes to my children? (such as unsupervised play, room sharing and privacy, physical aggression, etc.)

- How am I going to make special, individual time for each of my children every week?
- How will self-care be supported for the whole family?
- What are the important house rules? How will I handle it if a rule is not followed?
- What are the limitations with my employer?
- Do I need therapy (or couples therapy) before becoming a parent? Do I want to establish a relationship with a therapist so I have them available to work with as needed in the future?
- For couples, what is our plan to make sure we are getting enough time together?

A FOSTER PARENT SHARED THEIR REFLECTION

"I wish I already had an established relationship with a licensed therapist as I initially dealt with secondary trauma, and then later, as I experienced primary trauma over the three years we were licensed."

Preparing the Kids in Your Home

Being a foster family isn't just life-changing for you but also for the children already in your home. Consider the following to make sure the kids in your home are ready to become a foster family.

- **Introduce them to the idea of a foster family** through books, social stories, and pretend play. *Sesame Street* has several videos on the topic that young children can find supportive. For older kids, you can start by asking them what they already know about foster care. You can use this as a place to build. You can also watch TV shows and documentaries about foster care together to spark conversation.

"What do you already know about foster care?"

"Do you know anyone in your school who is or was in foster care?"

"What was foster care like for them?"

Take care as you talk about how long the child will be in your home.

 "Kids will stay only for a short amount of time" may be misleading, as some youth remain in foster care for years.

- **Ask for their input.** Get their involvement in setting up the bedroom, picking out special gifts, or finding ways to help the children feel comfortable and welcome. Their early involvement can help lay the groundwork for continued collaboration throughout the foster care process.

"What are some ways that we could make new children feel welcome in our home?"

"How should we decorate their bedroom? What do you think they would like?"

"What are some things we could do together when the kids move in?"

- **Collaborate on boundaries and rules.** This conversation can be important for you to start to understand possible areas of concern with your children.

"What items do you feel comfortable sharing with other children? And what items do you want to keep to yourself?"

"What family activities or traditions are most important to you?"

"What do you hope stays the same with our family when we start fostering?"

"What are some ways we can introduce kids coming into our foster home to your friends? What are some things we should share vs. not share?"

- **Create a plan about what to do if they have worries or questions.** Intentionally or not, this process may introduce your children to new topics and situations. Having open communication as early as possible is fundamental to a positive foster family experience.

"What are some reasons a family might need help?"

"What questions do you have about kids who are in foster care?"

"What could you do if there's a tricky situation with one of the kids who moves in?"

- **Make a plan for individual time to spend together each week.** Brainstorm special things you can do together when children move in to stay connected.

"What are special things you like to do together with just me and you?"

- **Kids may need time to think about things. They may change their mind after a child moves in and they experience being a foster family.** Be open to them changing their mind in the future. The key here is to start the conversation and open the door for conversations down the road.

"Thank you for sharing with me how you feel about fostering. I want us to always be able to talk about things—*even the hard things*. It's okay if you change your mind about something; your voice and needs matter." You can come up with a code word, signal, or emoji that the kids can use if they are feeling uncomfortable or need your help.

A FOSTER PARENT FROM THE COMMUNITY SHARED

"We prepared our biological kids to understand the difference between equal and equitable. Everyone will get their wants and needs met in the way that makes sense for them. It will not look the same for everyone."

Tips for Single Foster Parents

Being a single foster parent can come with some unique challenges. This advice came from other single foster parents like you:

- Finding a support system is crucial. Identify people who can help with certain tasks, such as babysitting, fixing things around your house, running errands, organizing a meal train, helping with homework, etc.
- You may want to start with one child, rather than a sibling group, to make sure you have enough capacity and support.
- You can't swap with a partner when you are triggered, so having skills to help yourself regulate in the moment are really important.
- Find ways to make household tasks more efficient, such as grocery deliveries or pickups, decluttering (less to clean!), meal planning and prep (make extra for the freezer!), baskets and bins for quicker tidying, trash cans in more rooms of the house for easier cleanup, etc.

- Take plenty of notes about what is happening, since there is no one else witnessing specific behavioral or emotional needs.
- Having a flexible job can be really important, since it's on you to manage sick days, appointments, etc.
- It gets difficult, but know that you are such a special, safe place for these kids! Some youth do especially well with a single parent who gives them their full attention or in homes with fewer people. There are many benefits that's unique to single foster parenting. Thank you for signing up!

Finances

Each month foster parents receive a stipend that is meant to reimburse them for all of the expenses related to caring for the child. In some states, these stipends are sufficient and cover most of the costs of fostering, while in other places in the United States, the stipends are more limiting and don't cover everything needed for the child. This is why financial considerations before fostering are important.

Stipends are typically based on the age or the level of care needed for the specific child. For example, children who are disabled or have higher behavioral or emotional support needs may receive a higher stipend. Each state and county typically have a formula or way to determine the level of care and the associated stipend.

It's important to note that sometimes relatives/kinship providers have different requirements to receive stipends. Additionally, stipends may change depending on plans like guardianship or adoption.

Budget Template

The following budget template includes increased/additional expenses you may not yet have thought about. Do some research to estimate the costs for these categories in your area and use the budgeting template on the next page as a starting point.

Consider the following:

- Does the stipend cover the estimated expenses? If not, do I have funds available to cover costs?
- Do I have a financial plan if the monthly stipend is delayed a few months?

> Getting set up in the payment system may take some time. Consider direct deposit methods to avoid additional delays or issues with the mail. Ask your worker if that's possible.

- How much can I spend out of pocket to meet the child's needs?
- How much unpaid time off work can I afford?
- What is my financial limit, and what do I do when I hit this limit?

> It can be helpful to have separate accounts for the foster care stipends. This helps with proper accounting and budgeting. If there is ever a question from the worker or parent(s) about how you are using funds, it's much easier to document how you spend the money when the account is fully separate.

CATEGORIES	MONTHLY BUDGET	EXAMPLES
Food		Foster parents can access benefits from WIC and kids may qualify for free food from the school district.
Increase in utilities		Such as gas, electric, water, streaming services, phone
Gas to visits and appointments		Sometimes you can request transport assistance or mileage reimbursement, especially for longer trips. You can also request busing for youth to remain at their home school.
Hair Care / Personal Care Expenses		Haircuts, soap, shampoo, period products, etc.
Clothing, Shoes, Accessories		Some counties will require you to submit receipts for a specific amount spent each month. You may be able to get support at Foster Closets (free shopping centers for foster families).
Allowance		Each county will have different requirements for allowance for kids by age. You can typically find this directive by searching online.
Activities		This includes typical childhood activities like extracurriculars, family outings, gifts for friends' birthday parties, etc. Some counties may have extra funds for these items or some courts will approve funding for things that support normalcy.

CATEGORIES	MONTHLY BUDGET	EXAMPLES
Misc. Kid Supplies		Water bottles, school supplies, booster seats, craft supplies, over-the-counter medications, etc.
Daycare		Some counties will cover the cost of daycare or afterschool programs, but it can vary and also depend on your work hours and availability within programs.
Other		Will be depending on the age and needs of each youth
Monthly Stipend		Update this number to reflect your monthly reimbursement
Budget		A total of the above
Leftover Emergency Fund / Savings		The difference between the stipend and your budgeted amount. This could be used for damages / broken Items, loss of work, savings for birthdays/holidays, babysitters for date nights, etc. You can put extra onto a gift card to use later, allow the child to save or spend, or give back at reunification.

Extra Expenses or Surprises

Foster parents in my community have experienced many surprise expenses that go above and beyond the typical daily expenses. Here is what they've shared with me, so that you won't be surprised!

- **Full wardrobe:** Some kids arrived at foster homes with zero clothing and toiletries, and some noted that kids were not even wearing shoes.

Don't assume a child coming from another foster home will arrive with a full wardrobe. Unfortunately, some foster parents misuse the stipend and do not meet the child's needs. If a child arrives from another foster home without clothing, alert the worker.

- **School supplies:** This may include backpacks, tech, lunch boxes, and water bottles. Even when kids arrive in the middle of the school year, sometimes everything still needs to be purchased. Usually, foster care nonprofits do a back-to-school backpack drive for foster families, but if a child moves in midyear, foster families may miss this donation opportunity.
- **Seasonal items:** These are items like winter jackets, heavy boots, snowsuits, swimsuits, life vests, goggles, swim lessons, summer camp, etc.
- **Vehicle expenses:** Visits and appointments may be far away, causing additional wear and tear on your car or higher fuel or charging costs. If you foster teens, this may include driver's ed classes or rideshares for the youth to use around town.
- **Daycare expenses:** Some daycares have deposits, supply fees, extended-hour fees, etc. In some places/situations, the county does not reimburse childcare, and it is the responsibility of the foster parent.

- **Medical needs:** This may be specialized medical items like formulas that aren't covered by WIC, braces, medications, or equipment not covered by Medicaid.
- **Special requests:** Kids may want to participate in special activities or have hobbies that require purchasing equipment (like sports or musical equipment).
- **Sensory items:** Youth may need sensory items like weighted blankets, sensory swings, compression shirts, fidgets, etc.

Schedule and Boundaries

Understanding your personal limits ahead of time can help you work through difficult moments that may come your way. As you work through these thought starters, it's important to also keep in mind that flexibility is key to foster parenting. The system is tough, and everyone working in it is under their own constraints and intensive workloads. There may also be confusing or unfair protocols that foster parents must work within. As you define your boundaries in this section, please keep in mind that flexibility will need to be baked into your plans to be a successful foster parent.

Ask yourself (for the purpose of this exercise, this does not include emergency moments):

- When will I be available for texts, calls, and appointments? How firm is this boundary? How will I hold this boundary if a parent or worker contacts me outside of this time frame?
- How will I keep track of all of the appointments? What system works best for me? How will I include the entire family in the schedule?

- When will I have dedicated individual time with my permanent children each week?
- When will my partner and I have time together?
- How will I spend time on my personal self-care, interests, and goals?
- How much driving am I willing or able to provide?
- How much time can I take off from work, or how flexible are my working hours to accommodate surprise daycare pickups, appointments, visits, etc.?
- For summertime placements, do I have a plan for childcare or supervision of youth who can't be left alone at home?
- How will I know when I am being spread too thin?
- What is the plan when I've hit my limit?

An example to consider: The parent(s) of the children in your care may be actively involved and pursuing reunification. They may reach out to you often, during the day or night, with questions about how their children are doing. The worker may tell you that many of their foster parents handle the visits with parents and ask you to supervise the parent visits three days a week for a few hours each time. They may be short-staffed and can't handle supervising all of the visits, so they want your help with this. And in addition, the child may have siblings at another foster home, and the other foster parent may not be willing to facilitate the sibling visits. As you can see in this example, there may be many scheduling needs to map out. This is not an impossible situation, but it likely requires strategy and support to meet everyone's needs (including yours).

Family Boundaries

Some families have rigid rules and may find some foster parenting scenarios difficult (but not always impossible with a plan!). It's good to identify ahead of time any strong immediate-family boundaries so that you have a plan and can think of some creative solutions for how to meet the child's needs, while also honoring your family's.

- What are my family's most important traditions and cultural needs?
- How can we incorporate and celebrate the new kid's family traditions and cultural needs?
- Does anyone in our family have required dietary or health needs?
- How will we support these needs in our home while balancing the required needs of the youth we care for?
- What are our family's religious needs?
- How will we incorporate and celebrate the new child's religious needs?
- How will we provide childcare if the child does not wish to participate in any of our religious or cultural traditions?
- What will our pet(s) need to maintain safety? What are the rules related to our pet(s)?

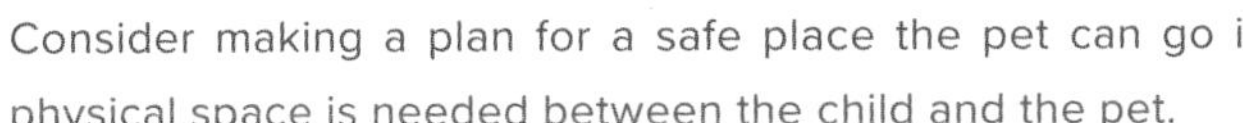

Consider making a plan for a safe place the pet can go if physical space is needed between the child and the pet.

An example to consider: Your family is vegan, and you have no animal products in your home. You welcome a young child into your home who is most comfortable eating meat products and drinking cow's milk. Even when you try to find suitable vegan alternatives, the child refuses to eat these alternatives. In this example, the foster family's job is to ensure the child has their needs met, including getting enough to eat. This family would need to find a way to meet the child's needs and their own needs at the same time, or they may need to put constraints on which kids they say yes to fostering.

Gathering Your Community

A solid support system isn't a nice-to-have; it's a must-have. Your licensing worker likely will ask about this, too, as having a support system is a contributing factor in getting approved to foster.

A MEMBER OF THE COMMUNITY SHARED THIS SENTIMENT

"Having go-to people for babysitting, venting, advice, or just showing up with dinner was crucial—especially in the first few chaotic weeks."

Close friends and family: Your close friends and family are typically the people who will interact directly with the kids who come through your home. They (hopefully) will also be your rock and your steady support through all of the seasons of foster care. Because of this, it's important they have some basic knowledge of how foster care works.

You can engage your friends and family by creating a private forum to have these discussions and update them about what is going on. Some foster parents send emails or use other online tools to privately connect. Each department will have different privacy rules. Generally, information can't be posted publicly about kids you are caring for, so be sure you have a clear understanding of these rules.

Here's an email template for how you can get this conversation started! Adapt this with your own unique style and tone.

To our friends and family,

We have some news to share—we are officially becoming foster parents! The next few months will be very busy with classes and getting our home ready. We hope to be licensed by the summer, at which point, we anticipate getting calls quickly about children who need a home.

If you're interested in staying in the loop about our foster care journey, please let us know. We can share some dos and don'ts when it comes to supporting the kids in our home, updates about when children move in and out, and we can let you know about ways you can help if you're interested.

Thank you in advance for being a part of our support system!

Extended network (work and acquaintances): This group of folks may not be privy to the day-to-day or interact with the children that come into your home, but they can still be important people in your life. This group could include your extended family, coworkers, workout group, or religious community. By looping them in to your plans to foster, you may find that someone in your extended network also fosters, or perhaps they are connected to child welfare in some way.

It can also be a chance to get ahead of any uncomfortable moments. "You may see me at our meetups with different children. Please don't mention foster care or the fact that they're newly in our home. Please try to do your best to treat them like the other kids who join."

When an uncomfortable moment happens: If you don't want to share or answer a question, or if someone says something that isn't exactly respectful or appropriate, here are some responses you can give:

"We are keeping those details private."

"Now is not a good time to talk about that."

"We don't have an answer for that—we live in the unknown most of the time."

"I appreciate you caring so much about them. Right now, that part of their story is private, and one day they may want to share it themselves."

"That is actually a common myth about foster care and not true."

"When you said that earlier, it could be interpreted differently than what I think you meant. I'd prefer if you..."

"I know you are trying to connect with them, but that topic is off-limits."

"I know you are trying to help, but next time, please come get me, and I can step in."

"I appreciate you taking the photo, but please don't post that on social media."

Work considerations: You may want to talk about fostering with your employer ahead of time. Both Chris and I worked full-time. I found this to be very difficult, but not impossible. Ask your employer about these topics:

- FMLA (Family and Medical Leave Act) benefits
- Paid leave opportunities
- Flexible schedule
- Flexibility with working remotely
- Childcare benefits

If you work with children or in a job that requires background checks or mandated reporting, please take a look at chapter 17 for information about false child abuse allegations and how that may impact your work.

Foster parent friends: If you are brand-new to the foster care community, you may not know anyone else who fosters. That's okay! Many of us start there. But don't let it end there. Your foster friends are important people in your life. They will get it in a way that no one else will. Their advice will likely be more actionable, and they probably have trauma-conscious parenting skills that can be helpful for babysitting or providing respite.

Ways to meet other foster parents:

- At foster parent training classes (in virtual classes you can post to the chat!)
- Foster parent support groups
- Nonprofit volunteer opportunities
- Foster care–related community events
- Asking your licensing worker to connect you with foster parents in your neighborhood/area
- Online foster parent groups for your county or state
- At your local foster closet

3
Getting Your Home Ready

TL;DR: Set your home up with safety and connection in mind, and don't forget to get kid-friendly items for all spaces in your home. Keep extra supplies on hand to be ready for a call at any time and to ensure you can accommodate support needs for all kids.

Setting up your foster home can feel like an overwhelming endeavor, especially if you are like me and started fostering without having any parenting experience! In this chapter, I will break it down for you so you can be prepared to support a variety of needs that kids may have as they enter your home.

Foster Home Setup Essentials

- ☐ **Get the checklists from your department:** Ask for the home inspection checklist and/or the fire inspection checklist early in the process so you can plan for any potential home updates that will be needed and research their costs. These checklists will cover the bare minimum requirements to pass the home inspection.
- ☐ **Make it easy to navigate:** Make sure the whole house is well lit at night, and consider putting signs or labels on doors and drawers so that

it's easy to navigate. Use visuals to indicate specific instructions, as needed.

- ☐ **Focus on safety:** While your home inspection checklist should include many safety features in your home, it's good to do a walk-through of your house to make sure that all areas where a child could get hurt have been identified and modified as needed. This could mean anchoring furniture, swapping out existing rugs with nonslip rugs, adding corner protectors on low tables, and moving or locking up items that could be dangerous if ingested (such as medications, chemicals, cleaning supplies, or batteries). Additionally, don't forget to put together an emergency kit that includes food and supplies for all ages, including infants.
- ☐ **Put away breakables or valuables:** Kids are kids. Things that you think are decor may look like toys to kids. Assume that things that are out will get touched and played with and (potentially) broken. When you add possible meltdowns into the mix, you want to be confident that you will be able to show up fully for the kids and not be distracted by Grandma's crystal bowl on the table, which might get broken. A good rule of thumb is that until you get to know the kids in your home, you may want to move breakable or sentimental items out of reach or fully put them away.
- ☐ **Make space:** Kids' items and supplies take up a lot of space, and you also want the children in your care to feel like there is room for them in your home. As you are rearranging and decluttering, make sure you are being mindful of space for the kids. This could be a place for their photo on the wall, room on the fridge for their artwork, a drawer they can use in the bathroom, a secure space for them to keep sentimental items, an extra chair at the dinner table or in the living room.

- ☐ **Make it kid friendly:** You'll also want to remember to pick up kid-friendly dishware, serving ware, cups, and step stools for handwashing. Incorporate colorful blankets, books that feature diverse skin colors, backgrounds, and/or disabilities on the covers, and toy bins ready to be explored. You can stretch this to the front of your home, as well. It can be intimidating for a child to walk up to a stranger's home, but a festive doormat or yard decorations can show that this is a place where kids are welcome! Add a visible symbol of LGBTQ+ pride (like a Progress Pride Flag) to signal to everyone entering your home that it's welcome to all. Don't forget to kidproof your technology by creating kid accounts and adding restrictions to all technology in the home.
- ☐ **Start your organization systems:** Start laying the groundwork for organization of paperwork in your home (corkboards, binders, filing systems, etc.). You'll have monthly paperwork and core documents for the child that you'll need to keep for easy reference (medical summaries, IEP (individualized education program), court documents, etc.). Where in your home will these documents be stored and organized? You will also need to find a way to track the children's items (such as toys from their parent(s) they no longer play with, clothing items that are in good condition but no longer fit, important schoolwork, etc.).

> As a nice-to-have, you may want to put a bunch of premade meals in the freezer for the kids and for yourself!

A Closer Look at the Foster Care Bedroom

You may hear advice that you should set up the bedroom in a neutral tone, allowing kids to personalize and make it their own after they move in. Maybe someone told you to leave it relatively empty so they can fill it with their own items. Or perhaps you thought you should keep things plain so it could work for any age or any gender.

Following this advice may leave the foster care bedroom looking stale or even *institutional.* I'd like to suggest some alternative considerations. Here are some things to keep in mind as you set up this space:

- **Warmth and comfort:** Colorful tones, gentle lighting, and soft textures can create an environment that is welcoming and caring. Consider the use of patterns (like polka dots, stripes, waves, leaves) or a colorful accent wall to add dimension to the room. Include affirmations on the walls or mirror that can help any child feel seen. Soft comfort items like stuffed animals or loveys can immediately put a child at ease.
- **Functionality and ease:** Furniture pieces that have built-in storage or convertible crib-beds can be really helpful as kids of all ages come and go. Don't forget to add labels or signs to help kids find what they need in the bedroom. If kids are sharing a bedroom, having ways to create privacy can be helpful too. This could be with a door hanger that lets people know that they would like privacy, separate dressers or desks, bed tents, or a room divider.
- **Supports and accommodations:** Throughout this book, I will share a variety of items that could be supportive of specific needs kids have. However, some of the most common support items include keeping some snacks in the bedroom, having access to TV or music in some way, weighted blankets, personal lighting, sound machines, and a rocking chair if you are fostering infants or toddlers. If there's room,

Wall decals to create a kid-friendly vibe that can be easily switched out for personalization

Weighted blanket or extra blankets for various needs

Soft and friendly items that can be used for comfort

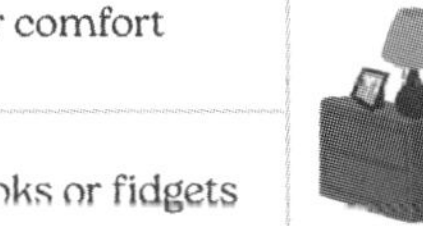
A variety of books or fidgets for connection or creating a calming space

Kid-friendly rugs for play, sitting, or rest can add warmth to the room

Desk for homework

Lights can completely transform and personalize the space

Snack box or mini fridge for kids who have food-related needs

A space for dimmer lighting options, water, sound machine, or music player

A rocking chair for bedtime or sensory support

Beanbag or comfy chair for a calming space

consider including books for connection time, a calming space (with a comfy chair with fidgets and other sensory supports), or a desk for homework time.

- **Choice and control:** There are many ways you can give the youth choice and control. It may not make sense on day one to offer all of these options at once (some youth may have trouble making decisions when they're unsure about you and the environment), but building in areas for them to personalize over time can be meaningful. Some examples:
  - Choice of bedding: Keep a few options on hand or have them shop for something they like.
  - Choice of wall decals: You can find these on sale and keep a variety of themes for them to choose from and decorate with. Posters can also work! Wall decals and posters can also be a safer option than framed photos hanging on the wall.
  - Moving around the furniture: For bigger spaces, you can offer that the youth can change things up. Make sure you tell them you would like to help move the heavy furniture so no one gets hurt.
  - Different lighting options: Offering color-changing LED strip lights or a star projector can completely transform a space. Having smaller lamps can provide different levels of brightness for the youth while they sleep.

Items to Keep on Hand

Below is a checklist to reference of items to keep on hand for your first placement or if you are restocking between kids (especially if you are providing emergency foster care).

- ☐ Kid's toothbrush/toothpaste (don't forget an infant toothbrush if needed!)
- ☐ Plenty of soap, shampoo, conditioner, face wash, deodorant, and other toiletries
- ☐ First-night clothing needs: socks, underwear, pajamas for the size of child you plan to foster
- ☐ Hair care items like brushes, combs, hair ties, bonnets, satin pillowcases, durags, and hair care products for a variety of hair textures and needs
- ☐ Pads, tampons, panty liners
- ☐ Free and clear laundry detergent
- ☐ Sensitive skin soaps and lotions
- ☐ Shelf-stable snacks/comfort food (see chapter 11 for ideas)
- ☐ New water bottle or nonspill sippy cup (to keep by their bed)
- ☐ Wipes (fragrance- and dye-free) for diapering or household cleanup, or body wipes for kids who may not feel comfortable showering right away
- ☐ Kids' over-the-counter medications and bandages (you may need a doctor's note to give OTC meds to a child, but it's good to have them on hand so you don't have to make a trip to the store while caring for a sick child!)

> Keep tags on so youth know that it is fresh and new for them. This also makes things easier to return!

Age-Specific Items

Infants:

- ☐ Baby carrier
- ☐ Stroller
- ☐ Baby enrichment: toys and loveys, play mat, board books
- ☐ Infant first aid items, diaper rash cream, and medications
- ☐ Rocking chair or glider
- ☐ Baby sun-protection hats and sunscreen (check with the pediatrician when it's appropriate to start using sunscreen for infants)
- ☐ Variety of bottles
- ☐ Variety of pacifiers
- ☐ Variety of diaper sizes
- ☐ Infant sleep sacks

> Note that some departments have stopped allowing swaddling without a doctor's note.

- ☐ Formula

> Many of the major brands offer free samples and coupons on their websites.

> You may want the predivided formula dispensers for easy transporting for bottle making at visits and appointments (or in the middle of the night!).

Young children:

- ☐ Pull-ups
- ☐ Potty-training seat
- ☐ Potty-training underwear
- ☐ Calm-down/safe spaces like a tent
- ☐ Educational toys

Older children:

- ☐ Welcome binder: written information about how to work things in the home, emergency hotlines/text lines, your contact information, Foster Child Bill of Rights, etc.
- ☐ Communication journal: for youth to share things with you that they may be too uncomfortable saying out loud. You should write the first entry.
- ☐ Safe shaving products: While some youth will be approved to use razors, some may not. You can offer electric razors or hair-removing lotions.
- ☐ Plenty of tech charging cables
- ☐ School and homework supplies, backpack, and lunch box
- ☐ Small lockbox: for their sentimental, precious items

> These boxes are important to hold family photos, letters from a sibling, etc., when the youth may be worried that another child in the home may take them. However, it's important to address the rules that unsafe items can't be stored in the box, and that you want to value their privacy while keeping everyone in the home safe.

Things for *You* to Use

- ☐ Diaper/visit bag with lots of compartments
- ☐ Quick-print cameras, like a Polaroid camera (this makes it easy to quickly post photos around the home of the new child)
- ☐ Lifebook or photo album (a new one for each child)
- ☐ Milestone-moment items such as a footprint or handprint craft, a memory box for the outfit they wore home from the hospital, a special box for teeth collected by the tooth fairy, etc. (parents may want these items)
- ☐ Organization system for paperwork (corkboard, folders, binders, journals, etc.)
- ☐ Helpful apps to download for your use:
    - Social stories apps: There's a variety of apps that will create social stories using your own images and voice. This is helpful when previewing a change or a more difficult appointment. It can also help if you are caring for a neurodivergent youth or a youth who does best with visuals.
    - FosterPower: A free and important app if you are fostering older youth! There are easy-to-understand descriptions of common child welfare processes, and there are also videos that cover so many topics for older kids in care (such as going to court, group homes, general advice, LGBTQ+ rights, medications, siblings, etc.).
    - CDC Milestone Tracker: This is a great way to know where the child is developmentally and can support you as you advocate for services/therapy. Take these results to the pediatrician if you find they are not meeting milestones.
    - WIC apps: Helpful for navigating the WIC system if you are new to it! Make sure you are downloading the correct app for your

state/location. This will show which specific items you can purchase with the benefits.

- Translation apps: Helpful for communicating with youth or parents.

Stock Your Bookshelves

Books can be such a helpful tool in your foster parenting toolbox! They can help explain difficult situations in age-appropriate ways, be a way to connect and bond with youth, and open the door for deeper conversations.

Check out these kids' books about foster care:

- *The ABCs of Foster and Kinship Care* by Raquel McCloud, illustrated by Taylan McCloud
- *Families Change* by Julie Nelson, illustrated by Mary Gallagher
- *A Day or Forever, I'll Love You the Same* by Michelle Thompson, illustrated by Karina Galvan
- *Foster Care: One Dog's Story of Change* by Julia Cook, illustrated by Marcela Calderon
- *Home for a While* by Lauren H. Kerstein, illustrated by Natalia Moore
- *Kids Need to Be Safe* by Julie Nelson, illustrated by Mary Gallagher
- *Lily's Story* by Danielle Grace Ignace, illustrated by Frances Rose R. Español
- *Maybe Days* by Jennifer Wilgocki and Marcia Kahn Wright, illustrated by Alyssa Imre Geis
- *No Matter What* by Josh Shipp with David Teiche, illustrated by Yuliya Pankratova
- *What Is Foster Care?* by Jeanette Yoffe, illustrated by Devika Joglekar
- *Adoption Is Both* by Elena S. Hall, illustrated by Lara Norris
- *Being Adopted* by Amy Wilkerson

- *The Day Lily Turned (un)Invisible* by Daniela Coats, illustrated by Helda Clara

A few considerations:

- You may not want to read heavy foster care–related books at bedtime. These topics may be triggering.
- Consider stocking nostalgic books or books that have been around for generations (like *Goodnight Moon*). These books may be found in the child's home, and so they may recognize them on your shelf.
- Read kids' books about foster care or heavy topics by yourself before reading them to the child. You may find that the story does not properly align with what the child is facing or the ending may not be realistic for the child in your home.
- Consider making your own book about your family! Introduce yourselves, include photos and pictures of things you like to do, and make it cheerful and friendly. It doesn't have to be beautiful or professional! This can be such a wonderful way to find common interests with younger kids who enter the home.

Purposeful Games and Toys

Some things I didn't realize I would need were specific games and toys that helped with foreshadowing, teaching a new skill, regulation support, and connecting/bonding. You'll find these items in many foster homes:

- **Playhouses and figurines:** a way to explain foster care situations or upcoming changes.

- **Modular kid furniture:** like the Nugget—to create calming areas, to make a fort to hide in, or to be used as a crash pad to let out energy.
- **Sensory items:** These may seem like toys to an untrained eye, but they are tools to support regulation throughout the day. They include fidgets, sensory socks, swings, or hammocks; weighted items (like blankets, lap pads, or stuffed animals); slime, Play-Doh, and kinetic sand.
- **Bubbles:** can also be used to teach about taking deep breaths.
- **Arts and crafts supplies:** a creative outlet and a calming activity.
- **Board games:** a way for the whole family to connect and bond.
- **Picture charades:** not just a fun game, but the picture cards can be used to communicate more clearly for children who are nonspeaking or if you have having trouble understanding what they need.
- **On-the-go games:** like Spot It, Uno, or a deck of cards, great for long waits at appointments.
- **Pretend doctor's kit, dentist's kit, play kitchen, and dress-up clothes:** used to foreshadow and explain a variety of appointments.

Sourcing Everything

If you are a first-time parent, you likely have no supplies in your home. It can be expensive to get fully stocked and ready to foster. Here are some ways you can source items for your home and for children placed with you:

- **Have a community gathering (similar to a shower):** Yes, it's a thing! But they are different from baby showers in many ways. They are similar in that you spend time with your friends and family, eat, play games, and collect items for your home. It's different, though, because you don't know the exact age or gender of the child you will be caring for, so the items on your wish list may differ from typical baby registries. The conversations may be more focused on how foster care works, answering questions, setting expectations with friends and family, and talking about the needs of families impacted by foster care. I recommend including the following items on your gift registry:

  - » Bulk items that will be needed for the first twenty-four hours
  - » Convertible furniture items that will work for a variety of ages and weights
  - » Memberships to the local zoo, museums, or indoor play places
  - » Gift cards for food delivery services, grocery stores, or family-friendly entertainment
  - » Home-safety items like child locks, cabinet locks, fire extinguishers, etc.
  - » Duffel bags for children to take their personal items with them to the next place when/if they leave your home

- **Ask for donations:** I found that most of my friends who were already parenting had plenty of items stored that they were excited to give to us. We had the space in our home to take in most items, and I labeled storage tubs based on age.
- **Join your local Buy Nothing group (or similar):** There are often Buy Nothing groups you can find on Facebook, where people give away items they no longer want for free, or you can post about an item you need. This is a great way to collect a ton of items, including furniture, clothing, toys, books, and other supplies.
- **Find your local foster closet:** Source this early so you know where it is located and what types of items it can potentially help with. You

likely will need to have the youth placed with you to have access to this shop.

- **Create an ongoing wish list:** Something that many foster parents do is create a wish list of ongoing needs for their foster homes. Friends and family can see the list at any time and purchase items as they wish.

4
Saying Yes (or No)

TL;DR: While saying yes will always be a leap of faith, asking the right questions ahead of time is important to ensure you have the capacity to help. Be prepared with your list of questions to ask during a placement call. Meet and greets and a welcome kit can help ease the transition.

You've spent so much time getting ready to foster, and now it's time for the final preparations.

Placements

Departments and workers will handle placing children differently depending on where you are and their communication preferences in reaching out to possible foster homes. You may get a text or email at first with very basic info, and then a follow-up call to discuss specifics. You may also just get a phone call, and in those situations, it can feel a bit more rushed, as workers are trying to find a home as fast as possible, so the youth doesn't have to sit in the office waiting.

Question Topics

You may have one hundred questions you want answered about the child, but the reality is you may get very little information about them or their situation. I recommend taking this long list below and highlighting the things that matter the most to you and your family. You will not be able to get clarity on everything, but I included many topics for consideration.

Basics:

- Gender
- Pronouns
- Birth date
    - » Ask for their birth *date* rather than their age. Workers are human, and sometimes their age is calculated wrong. They may also be arriving very close to their birthday.
    - » Understand that kids may be with you for over a year. Think about if you have space in your home or availability to meet their changing needs as they age.
    - » Remember that their biological age does not necessarily reflect their emotional or developmental needs. For example, a four-year-old may need pull-ups, ask for a bottle of milk, and need to be rocked to bed at night.
- Cultural/religious needs
    - » This may impact things like language(s) spoken, dietary restrictions, hair care needs, holidays, etc.
- Reason for removal or moving homes
    - » If they are coming from another foster home, ask to speak with the current caregiver to get more day-to-day information.
    - » You may not get the full story if the child is coming from another home. Get curious and recognize that there is often more to the story.

School:

- Grade in school
- School they currently attend
    - » There may be transportation services provided by the county that would allow the youth to remain at their home school. Ask about this!
    - » Ask if their siblings also attend this school (if they aren't being placed together). Sometimes school is the only time they may see their sibling.
- IEP, 504 plan, or early intervention services

History:

- Length of time in foster care
- Number of foster homes or group homes they have lived in
- Siblings and where they are placed (if not placed together)

Baby-specific:

- Suspected or confirmed exposure to substances
- Option to visit them in the hospital/NICU
- Anticipated discharge date

Medical:

- Current injuries
- Diagnoses
- Allergies
- Medications
- Specialized medical care needed

- Toilet training
    - » Keep pull-ups on hand if fostering younger children. You may find that upon moving into your home, they regress in their ability to use the toilet.

Visitation

Typically, visitation plans are only established if the child is already in foster care and the judge has ordered a visitation plan.

- Visit schedule (day, time, duration, location)
- Visit type (call, video, in person)
    - » In some places, phone calls are not formally ordered by a judge, but instead, it's expected for foster parents to facilitate parent-child phone calls on a regular basis. Ask the worker about the policies and procedures around phone calls.
- Transportation plan
- Visit supervisor (if visits are monitored)
- Visits with other relatives
    - » These may not be court ordered, but the worker may know of relatives or siblings who wish to visit with the youth. It's good to factor this into your plans.

Placement Type

- Emergency/short-term need
    - » If you are only available for a specific amount of time, make sure

you tell the worker the date you will no longer be able to care for the child. After they are placed, reiterate this boundary in writing.

- Current status of the case or case plan (e.g., parents working toward reunification, termination of parental rights [TPR] has occurred, moving to relatives)
- Native American, tribal affiliation or Indian Child Welfare Act (ICWA) status

Support Needs

- Developmental considerations
- Behavioral or emotional needs
- History of running away, taking things, harming or fear of animals, substance use, etc.
- Trauma triggers or considerations

A note about behavioral and emotional needs: You may feel less certain about being able to care for a child when you hear about their behavioral or emotional needs. I encourage you to pause and consider more about the nuances.

An example to consider: You may be told that the youth "has a history of running away." I would wonder: *Why do they leave? What do they need? Where are they going? Do they have an undiagnosed disability?* You may not get answers to these questions, but there's likely more to the story. Perhaps they need one-on-one care and more nurturing, closer supervision, flexibility in seeing friends, more family time, a different therapeutic team, help with emancipating, time with their sibling, etc. Remember, our job is not to "fix" a child. They don't need to be "fixed." They need to be heard, supported, and nurtured, and ultimately, they need a foster parent who can teach them, and advocate for their needs and safety. With that said, it is okay to not accept a child based on their behavioral or emotional needs if you do not feel equipped at this time. I share so you can consider and have an open mind when it comes to labels that can be misleading or harmful.

If you are uncertain: While workers may want an immediate yes from you, if you are not fully certain, you may be able to ask to speak with the child's worker or the current caregiver, request a meet and greet with the child, or first provide respite for the youth. In some situations, these things can be accommodated and can help ensure placement stability in the future.

Saying No

You may feel pressure or guilt when you hear about the child's situation, but remember that it's usually better to say no now than to say no later because you can't meet the child's needs. You may want to say no if any of the following applies to your situation:

- You have upcoming work or travel obligations
- You don't have space for all siblings

- You can't meet their cultural or religious needs
- You don't have childcare lined up
- You are still grieving the last child who left your home
- Not all of your family members want to keep fostering

If you aren't getting calls about kids in need of placement, this could be happening for a variety of reasons: It could be that there is no need right now for homes—which is good news! Let the placement worker know that you are available for respite. It could also be that the placement team doesn't know you have availability. Call the placement office or worker, and let them know you have room in your home. Lastly, perhaps your parameters are too strict and don't align with the kids who need a home in your county. Consider widening your age range or being open to sibling groups. You can also get certified to provide treatment foster care.

Meet and Greets

We actually had a meet and greet for the first children we fostered. This typically takes place when the current foster parent has disrupted or the youth is moving from a group home/treatment facility into a foster home. It's a way to help ease the transition, break the ice, and ensure fit. I wish I had been more prepared for what to expect and how to support in this situation. Consider the following if you are meeting youth before formal placement:

- If you are meeting via video chat, be prepared to show them around your home and their room, and you can also consider showing them around the neighborhood.
- If meeting in person at a facility, ask if you can bring any activities or food. If meeting at a park or the current foster parent's home, you can ask what would make sense for you to bring. Activities or snacks to share can be a good way to ease into the initial meet. Activities can include bubbles, coloring book, Frisbee, ball, etc.
- Try not to interrogate the child or fire off a bunch of questions. Make space in the conversation for them to ask questions too. This is a way to show them that their feelings, needs, and voice are important to you.

> For some kids, closed-ended questions can be an easier starting point. "Which do you like better, going to the beach or swimming in a pool?"

- If you have multiple meetups before they move in, you can deepen the questions/topic areas over time and understand some of their needs as you prepare for them to move in. For example, "What helps you feel better when you are having a bad day?" "What's something you want to learn how to do?"
- Be careful about what you discuss in regard to planning and timing for them to move in with you. Plans may change or moves may be delayed.
- Understand that these initial meetups do not necessarily reflect how it will be when they move in full-time. This is a "getting to know you"

phase, so take these moments and conversations as a place to begin. Be open to the youth changing their mind and preferences once they move in.

You've said yes... Now what?

It's time for some last-minute preparations! You may have a few hours, or you may have a few days. In your final moments of preparation:

- Check your supply closet and make sure you have enough clothing and supplies for the first twenty-four to forty-eight hours. Head to the store to pick up needed items or ask a friend to pick them up for you if you are strapped for time.
- Notify work so they know what's going on and what they can expect from you this week.
- Send a quick text or email to your community of support: 💬 "We just said yes to a fourteen-year-old girl. She'll be arriving in a few hours."
- If a friend or family member is offering to help in the coming weeks, say yes! Or if they ask what they can do to help, suggest dropping off a meal, running an errand for you, or even just asking them to check in on you over the next few days or weeks.
- Get a welcome kit ready (see below for more info).
- Pop some chocolate chip cookies into the oven, order pizza, or make some mac and cheese (and make yourself some coffee if you need it!).
- Breathe.

Welcome Kit

A basket or tray filled with items is a great way to help a child feel considered and welcomed. You can include…

- Shelf-stable snacks (see chapter 11 for examples)

> Some foster parents choose to stock a mini fridge in a bedroom for teens. Keep a covered trash can in their bedroom to maintain cleanliness if the youth is allowed to eat in their room.

- Coloring books with a new set of crayons or colored pencils, depending on age
- Journal with new pens

- New water bottle
- Flashlight or handheld light
- Hygiene items: toothbrush, toothpaste, hairbrush, hair ties, shampoo, conditioner, soap, period products, lotion, face wash, lip balm, etc.
- Comfort items: sensory/fidget items, stuffed animal, fuzzy socks, slippers, fuzzy blanket
- Welcome letter or a communication journal (see below)

You may also want to have a duffel bag for their items in case they arrive with their belongings in a trash bag or grocery bags. Some youth may not want to immediately unpack, and that's okay, but you can offer them a duffel bag to use instead of plastic bags.

Welcome Letter or Communication Journal

If you are fostering older youth, it may be helpful to include a short note saying hello to them. Some foster parents choose to offer a communication journal to older youth, as a way to talk about things that may be hard for them to say out loud. Here's a letter template to use as a starting point for you:

Hi, Madison,

Welcome to our home. We are Laura and Chris, and our cat's name is Penelope.

We've put together this basket for you, so please help yourself! There are also more supplies in your closet, like blankets, sheets, towels, and stuffed animals. You can use whatever you need. In the bathroom, there's a drawer with your name on it. We stocked it with some basic items, but we can talk more about the brands you like to use. If you'd like, we can go to the store together to pick up supplies, clothing, and snacks you like to eat.

I know that this has been a hard day. We are here to listen and answer any questions you may have. Even if we don't know the answer, we will do our best to find out. We can talk, text, or you can write questions down in this journal. We know that sometimes it's easier to write things down rather than talk. You can slip this under our door, and we will get back to you soon.

We care about your needs and are here to help however we can. We look forward to having you here and getting to know you better.

Laura and Chris
(Include phone numbers if they have their own phone.)

Part 2

Supporting Youth Inside Your Home

I signed up to help a child *heal*...

...but I realized that my role was to be a *safe place to land.*

5

Hi, there. Let's talk about the first week with a new child.

TL;DR: The first week will have unique challenges as kids get set up in your home. Take it slow, moment by moment, and tune in to the kid's needs at each turn. Don't forget to let your community know and check in with your permanent kids to make sure their needs are met too.

All your training has led to this moment: The child has just arrived. The next few moments, days, and weeks will be an important time as you get to know the child, meet their initial needs, and get them set up within the system and your home.

Even if the child is coming from another foster home, you may be surprised how little has been arranged for them. Each child deserves attention and care. Thank you, in advance, for saying yes and stepping into this child's life during this traumatic time.

A ton of "firsts" are about to happen. For this chapter, I've broken them into the first day and the first week.

It's important to be mindful that the first days, weeks, and even months, are the "getting to know you" phase for the child. Some call this the "honeymoon phase," which I tend to avoid using, because it focuses on the foster parent's experience (*Everything is good and easy, and the child is behaving perfectly!*) and doesn't acknowledge the difficulties kids face during this time. (*I don't want to break a rule because I am scared of what might happen. I don't know if I can be myself because I am worried about how my foster parent will react.*) Behaviors, supports, accommodations, and needs that you witness in this first phase of fostering may not last and may change as the child becomes more comfortable with you and your home.

The First Day

Saying Hello

Your first meeting may be at a meet and greet, picking up the child from the office or the hospital, or they may be dropped off at your home. Regardless of where the first "hello" takes place, here are a few things to keep in mind:

- **"Hi, there!":** Introduce yourself with your preferred name/nickname and pronouns. I don't recommend things like, ✖ "I'm your new Mom" or ✖ "You can call me Dad." You may be this to other kids in the home, and you can explain that, but *requiring* a child to call you Mom or Dad is not appropriate. With that, some children may ask to call you Mom or Dad, or may call you this without you prompting. This can happen for a variety of reasons. It can be age appropriate for young children to call adult caregivers "Mommy" or "Daddy"; the child may feel like that's what they are supposed to do in this situation; they may be trying to appease you; they may wish for a parent who takes care of them; or they may hear other kids in the home use certain terms so that's what they do too. You can meet the child where they are in this situation, and respond when they call you by these names. That being said, it is important to make sure they understand the distinction between your role and their parent.

- **Adjust to their tone:** If the child is sad, scared, or unsure, you can move slowly and gently. Older kids may want to sit in their room by themselves while you do paperwork with the worker. For younger kids, you can invite them to sit beside you or hold on to a stuffed animal. If they are antsy, excitable, dysregulated, or moving quickly, you may want to redirect them to an activity, TV show, snack, or outside play while items are brought in from the car. Be aware of your own tone too. I know for me, when I would meet kids for the first time, I sometimes was a little too excited and energetic. This may be overwhelming for some kids, so try to check yourself and take a few deep breaths before saying hello.
- **Offer choice and control:** Small moments of choice and control can be meaningful during this chaotic time. For example, 💬 "Do you want me to show you your room, or would you like to grab a snack first?"
- **Be mindful of pets:** Pets can be therapeutic and a great icebreaker, but not all kids are comfortable around them. If your pet is loud, jumps, does something that could startle someone, or runs or licks a lot, you may want to keep them outside or in a different space until you've had a chance to meet the kid and foreshadow meeting your pet.
- **For babies:** Greet them with a gentle or singsongy voice, move slowly, smile, and rock back and forth. Narrate what is happening as you bring them into your car or home.

Surprises and Mistakes

Removals can be chaotic and traumatic, and it can be difficult for workers to obtain accurate information about children during these times. I share this so you can be prepared and can consider ahead of time how you will adjust on the fly. Your flexibility, creative problem-solving, and advocacy skills will come into play in these situations:

- An additional sibling arrives that you hadn't planned on.
- The child arrives with a pet or a service animal without your prior knowledge.
- You have been told the wrong age or name, or this info is unknown.
- Certain medical needs were not disclosed or explained.
- Case-specific information given to you is not correct.
- They speak a different language than what you were told.
- They attend a different school than you were told.
- Developmental needs may be understated or overstated.
- The child may arrive on their birthday.

If you notice the error when the kids are present, try to maintain composure and be careful with what you say in front of them. It isn't their fault that a mistake has been made, so you don't want them to feel bad or blame themselves.

Paperwork

When the child arrives, the worker may want to sit down with you and review the child's case details, behavioral needs, stipend amount, and other necessary paperwork. For some kids, especially older youth, this can feel transactional or be triggering. Be mindful of whether the youth is in earshot and how information is discussed.

Initial House Tour

Show them around based on how they are feeling. For example, if they are disinterested or want to be alone, that's okay! You can show them around later. Allowing them some privacy while you finish up with the worker is fine.

As you introduce the different spaces to them, it may be best to only focus on the most important information. The details of living in your home can unfold over the next several days. They may also forget everything you say during the first tour—they are taking in a lot! It's important not to overwhelm them with a ton of rules or details. Instead, focus on what they need, and try to help them feel comfortable and safe. Consider pointing out the following on your home tour:

- **Their room and where they can put their things:** Let them know that this is where they will be sleeping tonight. Younger kids may be surprised by this, as they may not fully understand what foster care is, and an immediate panic or meltdown may take place.
- **The bathroom(s) and where they can keep their personal toiletries:** Show them where you keep extra items stocked (toothbrushes, toothpaste, shampoo, towels, period products, etc.) and tell them directly that they can help themselves. Consider opening boxes of supplies ahead of time, so they feel more welcome to take something.
- **Where the snacks and food are stored and if there are specific rules:** Consider keeping a "Yes" basket with snacks that can be accessed at all times. See chapter 11 for more info.

- **Safety systems in the home:** Such as locks on doors (bathroom, bedroom, outside), security systems, cameras, etc.
- **The most important rules and safety needs in the home:** Such as kids aren't allowed to leave the home without an adult. You can have collaborative house rule discussions later.
- **Where they can watch TV and charge their electronics:** Some youth may come with their own phone or electronics.

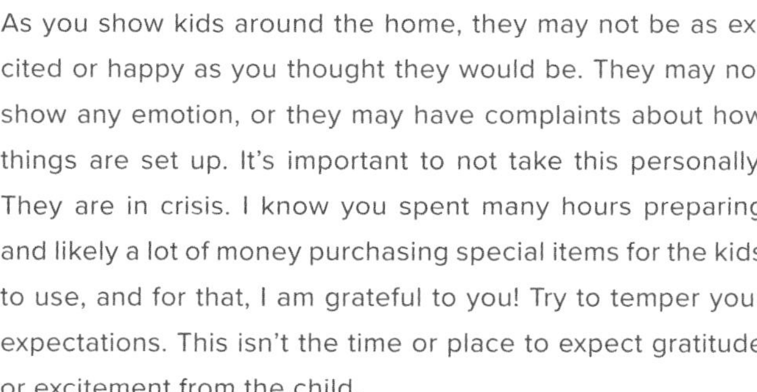

As you show kids around the home, they may not be as excited or happy as you thought they would be. They may not show any emotion, or they may have complaints about how things are set up. It's important to not take this personally. They are in crisis. I know you spent many hours preparing and likely a lot of money purchasing special items for the kids to use, and for that, I am grateful to you! Try to temper your expectations. This isn't the time or place to expect gratitude or excitement from the child.

Their Personal Belongings

Some children will arrive with multiple suitcases and bags, while others may arrive with nothing. Consider the following:

- **Privacy:** It's important to respect the youth's privacy. For younger kids, you can go through the items packed for them together. Some items may seem meaningless to you (like a random mismatched sock), but it could be a comfort item to the child. Watch their face and how they respond when you look through their things. For older youth, it often is not appropriate to go through their items, and sometimes it's completely against the youth's personal rights. Make sure you understand the protocol here. If you are concerned about anything, check with the worker. The worker should make you aware of any immediate concerns, like whether the children were exposed to substances (e.g., methamphetamine or fentanyl) or bedbugs, and if their items need to be washed or disposed of right away.

- **Washing clothes:** Washing the children's clothes may be necessary for sanitary reasons, but I would encourage you to move slowly and with purpose. Some children may wish to retain the scent of their home. They may also want to do their own laundry and may not feel comfortable with you touching their clothes. You also need to be careful with the language you use. It isn't their fault that they haven't showered or that their clothing is unwashed. You don't want them to feel like they are being blamed or that they are the problem.
- **Unpacking:** Some kids may not feel settled into your home for a while. They may not want to unpack and put their things into the drawers or closet. Try not to hurry this, as they may need some time to process what's happening.

Meet Initial Needs

This first day is an important time to show that you are able and willing to meet their needs. Try to accommodate even small requests, as this is the start of building a trusting relationship with each child.

You can have food already prepared to serve the kids or offer to order delivery from their favorite place. Even if they ask for fast food, I would encourage you to say yes. Each moment gives you a chance to learn about what they like and don't like. There's time to introduce other foods in the future. Right now, it's about meeting basic needs.

Kids may arrive very tired, which is understandable. Being removed from their primary caregiver is a significant trauma. Naps may be needed, or you can put the TV on for them to relax. Before older youth go to bed, you may want to talk about plans for the next day. Some youth will want to go to school so they can see their friends, have some normalcy, or see their sibling or favorite teacher. Some may want to take a mental health day and sleep in. It can really vary, so it's good to talk about it the night before.

For infants, you can start your time together with a fresh diaper, bottle, rocking, singing, or reading a book.

Bathing

Not all kids will feel comfortable bathing at your home right away. Remember, *you are a stranger, and everything is new*. While a warm bubble bath or shower may be desired, if they are resistant to bathing, it may be better to offer shower wipes or dry shampoo, or for them to wash up at the sink. And if it's all too much for the first day, that's okay. Showering and getting into fresh clothes can be something for tomorrow.

The First Night and Morning

Sleep on the first night may be unique. They could be terrified to be alone, want to sleep on the couch, have the TV on all night, or be with their sibling. They might need a walk in the stroller or a back rub to fall asleep. Other kids may want to be left alone with their door shut. If you are able, review:

- How to get in contact with you at night (call for you, come get you, use a doorbell system, text, etc.)

- Any strange sounds they may hear at night (e.g., the dishwasher or the air turning on)
- Where they can find extra pillows or blankets if they are cold or need to change their bedding (reiterate they can come get you for help)
- Where you will be at night and that you aren't leaving
- Where they can get a snack if they are hungry at night (if developmentally appropriate). You can also be sure they have a fresh glass of water or filled water bottle next to their bed.
- Where the bathroom is and be sure you say directly: 💬 "It's okay to get up at night to use the bathroom."
- What they can do if they have trouble sleeping (come get you, turn the TV on, read a book, color, etc.)
- Morning needs, such as what time and how they want to be woken up to get ready for school
- Any questions or worries

In the morning, consider having several different breakfast options available so they have a choice. Common kid-friendly breakfast items include cereal, toast, eggs, bacon or sausage, pancakes, toaster waffles, yogurt, banana, oatmeal, muffins or other pastries, or bagels and cream cheese. Some kids feel most comfortable eating food that they recognize, while others are open to trying new things. It really depends, and these smaller moments are how you will start to get to know them and their needs, and learn how to pick up on their verbal and nonverbal cues. It's also important to note that some kids may not have big appetites. The stress of entering foster care may make it hard to eat, so having a breakfast shake or granola bar to take with them on the road are great options.

Some kids may not know that it's okay to come out of the bedroom in the morning. For little ones, you can crack their door slightly when you get up in the morning so you can see in, or use a video monitor system (if it is allowed). If they are awake in bed, you can go in and say good morning.

Kids may not remember your name. Names are hard; that's okay! Remind them in the morning. "There was a lot going on last night when you arrived. My name is Laura, in case you forgot."

Hard Conversations

Children may have a ton of questions—many of which you won't know the answer to. It's better to be honest than to assume, lie, or dismiss their concerns or worries. Here are some common questions and a starting point for how you can answer. Be sure to adjust your responses based on their circumstances:

What is foster care?

- "Foster care happens when a child is removed from their mom or dad (or guardian). Kids live with a foster parent, like me. Kids go into foster care for many reasons, but it is never the child's fault. You did nothing wrong, and you are not in trouble."
- "I don't know the details about why you were removed from your parent(s). If you want to share anything with me that you saw or experienced, I am here to listen."

Who are you?

- "I'm Laura," "You can call me Laura," or you can come up with a nickname if the child can't pronounce your name.
- "I am a foster parent. I help take care of kids when their parents aren't able to. Sort of like a daycare worker or babysitter, but you stay at this house and sleep here."
- "I am helping your family out and will be taking care of you right now."
- "I am not replacing your mom, and I hope you can be back at home with your mom soon."

Where is Mom/Dad/my guardian?

- "I don't know where they are. If you want to talk about what happened, I'm here to listen, or maybe I can help you make sense of what happened."
- "As soon as I know what's going on, I will let you know."
- "The caseworker has been in contact with your parent(s). They are safe and okay. When I have more info, I will share it with you. That is all I know."

Can I talk to/see my parent(s)?

- "I hope you can talk to them soon. I am not in charge of that; the caseworker or the judge is. They decide when you can talk with/see your parent(s)."
- "I hope we can set up a visit soon. I will ask the caseworker when that can happen."
- "If they were here, what would you want to tell them/ask them? I can

write it down for you." (For younger kids, you can see if they want to draw a picture for their parent(s).)

Where are my siblings? Are they okay?

- "What are their names? I can ask the worker about them and try to set up a time to talk or at least get an update."
- "I don't know, and I am so sorry I don't have the answers. I will make it my priority to make sure the worker knows about them and that they are safe." (Physically write their names down to show the importance here.)
- "If I get in touch with their caregiver, what would you like me to tell them? Is there anything they need to know about your sibling?"

How long am I staying? When can I go home?

- "I don't know how long you will be here. As soon as I have more info, I will let you know."
- "Let's write this question down, so when the worker comes, we can ask together."
- "Sometimes kids stay for a short time, and sometimes it's longer. I'm sorry I don't have an answer."

Can you take me home?

- "I am not allowed to take you home. As soon as I have more information, I will tell you."
- "Is there anything from home you need? We can make a list, and I can ask the worker about it or pick up new stuff for you from the store."

Why can't I live with my friend or family member?

- "Right now, you cannot go to your grandma's. What is her name? I will let the caseworker know that you want to live with her right now. I don't know if it will be allowed, but I will ask and also let your attorney know."
- "You can invite your friends here; I would love to get to know them. Want to do a movie night on Friday? I can order pizza and pick up snacks."
- "Living with your friend's parents may not be possible, but I can certainly ask. What are their names and numbers, and I will tell the caseworker and attorney."

> These questions may be repeatedly asked—be patient as the kid processes what's going on.

> At some point early in the child's time with you, you want to make sure they know that you are a mandated reporter.
>
> "Part of being a foster parent is making sure kids are always safe. This means if I am worried about your safety or you tell me about an unsafe situation, I have to tell someone. This is so we can keep you safe or help keep other kids safe. If I feel you are in danger, I have to get other people's help." You may want to clarify *who* you will be telling (e.g., the child's worker). Also, it's important to remember that blanket statements like ✗ "I won't tell anyone" or ✗ "I promise not to tell" can be tricky. Sometimes foster parents must disclose information for investigation or safety reasons. Be mindful when using these phrases or making these promises.

Check In with Your Permanent Children

In the flurry of everything, don't forget to get that one-on-one time with your permanent children and answer their questions too. They may be wondering what's going on, how long the child will stay, and how life will be changing for them. It's okay if you don't have all the answers. Your attention is what matters.

> Take a deep breath—you did it. The first day can be heartbreaking, awkward, or exhausting. Or all of the above. You took the leap of faith and opened your home. This is the start of a new chapter. It may be short, or it may be long. Thank you for being part of the child's story.

The First Week

The first week is all about getting settled. You can start to establish some routines and schedules but just know that things are still in flux. Kids may not get comfortable for a while, and there may be a lot of trial and error when it comes to communication, preferences, food, and beyond. It isn't a time to be harsh with rules and consequences; instead, greet each moment as an opportunity to learn about them and for them to gently understand how your home works.

If you are a short-term emergency-care provider, the youth may only be with you for this week or a little longer. You are standing in the gap until a long-term placement is found.

In the first week, you might:

- Spend time getting to know the child

- Start getting organized and collecting info
- Attend the initial court hearing
- Take the children to the initial medical appointment
- Have a worker visit

Start getting to know the child:

- **Take them shopping:** Having kids shop the clothing racks and grocery aisles (in store or virtually) can be helpful in learning what they like and don't like. Going to a store is overwhelming for some youth, especially with a stranger. Using online shopping for clothes or a grocery delivery service may be a better experience for some.

> Don't assume gender or preferences. If they are with you, walk through all areas of the store (boys, girls, etc.). If they are not, ask what kinds of clothes or colors they like the most, and reiterate that they are free to choose what they are most comfortable with. Some kids may not feel comfortable discussing underwear, bras, etc., even if they need them. Be mindful of this.

- **Provide options:** Take out several books, open the pantry to display different snacks, or turn on Netflix and hand them the remote, and see what they gravitate toward. When you create these moments of choice, you can start to learn more about their interests and likes and dislikes. I've found that when asking kids, "What's your favorite…?" it can be difficult for them to come up an answer. "Show me" or "point to" or "your choice" moments can be more helpful than asking outright.

- **Be careful about overscheduling:** It can be really fun to go to the zoo or museum, but for the first week, you may want to limit outings since they are still adjusting (and so are you!). Instead, play in your yard, walk around the block, or visit your local park or library. It's good to build in normalcy, but you have to be mindful of their energy levels and all of the other meetings that will be happening soon.
- **Align on the "story":** For older kids who are attending school, it may make sense to align on how they want to introduce you to their friends and classmates. For example, are you a foster parent, family friend that's handling drop-off and pickup at school, their aunt, or their parent? Some kids don't want anyone to know they are in foster care, so this is something to discuss with the youth. Their feelings on this may change over time. There will be people you are required to tell about their foster status (like the school's enrollment office), so let the youth know that you will tell them when this happens.
- **Learn key words or phrases in their language:** If the child speaks another language, learn several words or phrases so you can communicate about their needs and desires. Use photos and translation apps to assist with this too.

Behind the scenes, start getting organized and collecting info:

- Write down the child's first and last name, age, birth date, health insurance information (if it's been set up yet), and the worker's name and number. You will likely be asked for this information over and over again, and at least for me, it took a little time to memorize it all! I hung this info on the fridge so I could easily reference it when someone called.

- Try to inventory what has come in with the child. This can be important so you can advocate for the child and ask the worker for additional funds for clothing and supplies, if needed. For older youth who don't want you to go through their personal belongings, you can ask them to tell you what they have and what they need.
- Thoroughly review all paperwork that is given to you. There can be important information about the youth's medical condition, allergies, school accommodations, behavioral or emotional needs, medication use, or details related to the case plan. Highlight holes or areas of concern for when you are able to connect with the child's professional team.
- Get to know their school. Some school districts have counselors or foster youth liaisons who can help connect them to resources at school or get them extra accommodations (such as changing their lunch schedule so they can have lunch at the same time as their sibling who might be in another foster home). The counselor can also check in on them and make sure they are doing okay with the big change.
- For babies and younger kids, take photos to eventually share with their parent(s). Parent(s) want to *see* that their kids are well cared for, especially kids who can't talk yet. Sending photos (with permission) is a way to show parents that their children are doing okay and help put them at ease. Upload them to a digital folder to share with the worker and parent, or consider printing pictures for when you meet.

- Update your community. Update and reshare the wish list you've shared with your friends and family in case they want to help with the move-in expenses! Consider emailing them to let them know what's going on.
- Consider clearing what you can from your schedule for the next month, such as pushing back work meetings or appointments. The next few weeks will likely be busy and exhausting, so it can be good to plan ahead for this as much as possible. You may qualify for FMLA leave or parental leave, and many foster parents take this time off when a new child moves in.
- Start collecting the contact info of everyone you speak to and who visits the child in the home. I liked to keep this information digitally on a Google Sheet so I could easily refer to it, share it with my husband, or share it with the worker (they often need all of the contact information too!). You may want to track:
    - » Agency worker/county worker and their supervisors
    - » Emergency worker
    - » Visit monitor and visit location, dates, and times
    - » Transport service provider
    - » Attorney/GAL (guardian ad litem)/CASA (court-appointed special advocate)
    - » School staff and teachers
    - » Daycare provider
    - » Mental health therapist
    - » Occupational therapist
    - » Speech therapist
    - » Physical therapist

» Relatives
» Siblings' foster parent or guardian

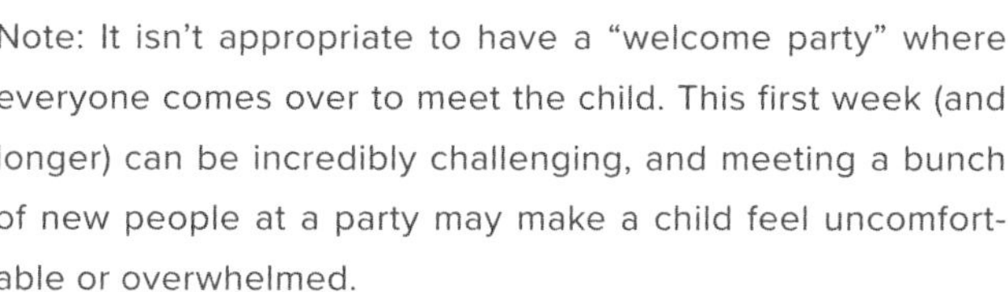

Note: It isn't appropriate to have a "welcome party" where everyone comes over to meet the child. This first week (and longer) can be incredibly challenging, and meeting a bunch of new people at a party may make a child feel uncomfortable or overwhelmed.

Initial Court Hearing

Usually in the first few days of a new case, there is an initial court hearing. Each county and worker will have different policies for whether the children attend and if foster parents can be present in the courtroom. If possible, go to the hearing and meet the child's attorney/GAL/CASA (if they have one) and their parent(s), and possibly listen to the court hearing so you can get a sense for what is going on. This background knowledge can be helpful as you begin to learn about the child in your care and their needs/trauma history.

If the youth is supposed to attend court (which is more common for youth once they reach a certain age), you can call the worker/advocate or the courthouse yourself to understand the specifics such as: Is transportation provided for the youth? What time is the hearing? What is the protocol for children and foster parents who wish to attend?

Initial Medical Appointment

In many places, children must be seen by a medical professional when they enter care for the first time. Sometimes the children see this person before they come to your home, and other times, foster parents are responsible for taking the kids to this appointment (usually within the first few days of placement).

If the child is unfamiliar with going to the doctor, you can use a toy doctor's kit, books, and videos to show them what to expect.

These appointments can be long. Consider bringing a tablet, activities, food, and drinks. You can ask the worker if their parent(s) can attend too. It may make sense to bring a friend if you have a sibling group, so that they can entertain one of the kids in the waiting room, if needed.

At these appointments, make sure you get printed copies of the visit summary or any form that is required by your department. Scan everything as well, in case you lose or give away your only hard copy. If the child has prescriptions, make sure you have all of the written instructions and any forms the school will need to administer the medications during the day. You may need written permission to use over-the-counter medications for each child. Make sure you know what is required by your county so you can get this permission at this visit. This can include OTC pain and cold medicine, allergy medicine, meds for tummy aches, etc. Additionally, get a copy of the child's vaccination records, as they may need them to enroll in daycare or school.

If the child has ongoing medical needs or is considered medically fragile, you can sometimes request special training so you can ensure you know how to properly meet their needs.

Worker Visit(s)

You can expect to see the child's worker in your home to sign paperwork. If you are with an agency, the agency worker *and* the county worker may both visit soon after the child is placed in your home. It can take some time for workers to be assigned. Call the office if you aren't hearing from anyone. In many places, there's a required time frame in which a worker must see a child in a new foster placement. Ongoing, monthly visits from workers are typical.

The initial worker visits are about gathering information and for them to get to know the child and you. It's great if some of these questions can be addressed before placement occurs, but often these details are still being worked out while the department is searching for a foster family. There may be a lot to cover. I've listed several question areas below, but go through this list before the worker visit so you can prioritize. It may not make sense to ask all of these in one visit:

Administrative details:

- What is the best way to reach you (phone, text, email)? And what is the best way to reach you in an emergency or for urgent matters?
- Who do I contact in the evening or weekends?
- How often will you visit the children? Will all of those visits take place at our home or someplace else?

Family:

- Is there anything I should know about the parent(s)? Are there any specific safety concerns? Are there rules about contact?
- What is the visitation plan (in person, calls, video)? Who is transporting the child, and what am I allowed or required to bring for them?
- Should parents be included in school meetings, doctor appointments, etc.?

- What language do the parents speak, and are translation services available?
- Are we having an icebreaker or team meeting with the parent(s) to meet each other?
- Have any other family members requested contact?
- Does the child have any siblings (including half, step-, or adult siblings)? If so, when and how can they see them?
- Is this placement short-term or potentially long-term? Are family members being considered for placement? Is reunification with parent(s) the goal?
- Does the child's family have any known tribal affiliation? What is their ICWA status? Has a home or plan been established?

Children:

- Will kids attend court hearings? If so, how is transportation arranged?
- Can you share anything that would be helpful for me to know about the removal or their history so I can best support any trauma triggers? Have the kids been in foster care before?
- Does the child have any history of substance abuse, self-harm, running away or eloping, or harming animals or other children?
- Are there any medical or mental health considerations or needs? Does the child have any prescriptions, allergies, disabilities, or other diagnoses?
- What is the child's home school? Is transportation provided? How am I allowed to engage with the child's teachers? Is there an IEP or 504 plan? Does the child need one? Who should request that?
- Are there LGBTQ+, cultural, or religious considerations to be aware of?

After the first week, you should have general information about the child and have started to get to know them and their needs. Are you getting any sleep? Have you eaten? It's okay to ask for help and call on your community to care for *you* too.

YOU CAN'T DO THIS IN ISOLATION, AS ONE FOSTER PARENT SHARES

"I really wish we had built a wider support network within the community. Our first few months with our first placement felt very isolating. Our preexisting community didn't know how to support us, and we couldn't really verbalize what we needed."

From here, the next month will likely still be a bit intense with meeting the kid's needs, enrolling in daycare or school, and a ton of appointments and phone calls.

These appointments can include:

- Advocate meeting (with their attorney, GAL, or CASA)
- Investigator meeting (if the child welfare department is investigating child abuse claims)

- Forensic exam (usually in cases of suspected sexual abuse but can also be required for instances of physical abuse or neglect)
- Initial dentist appointment
- Initial pediatrician appointment
- Icebreaker meeting or comfort call with parent (your first interaction with the parent)
- Initial parent visits
- Nurse visit (if there are injuries or medical needs)
- Mental health assessment and/or multidisciplinary assessment (to determine what services the child needs)
- Level-of-care assessment (to determine the appropriate stipend)
- Early intervention assessment (to determine if a young child needs developmental services)
- Child-family team meeting (formal meeting with professional team and sometimes parents too)
- Educational-related meetings (such as enrollment meetings)

Each worker and department is different, so it's likely you won't have *all* of these appointments or they will happen later down the road (or never). I share so you can be prepared.

I want to pause and acknowledge something: Your yes has changed more than the child's life. It's also changed yours. If you are feeling overwhelmed, anxious, nervous, or tired, those are all normal reactions when you've started a brand-new chapter in your life.

If you don't immediately feel connected with the child, that is also normal. It doesn't mean you are doing anything wrong. Allow yourself to grow in this relationship. ♡

When you say "Yes!" you aren't just saying yes to a child...

You are saying yes to...

parents workers court grandparents

therapists meetings trauma training teachers

medical professionals visits therapy appointments

siblings specialists a roller coaster reunification

paperwork accusations inspections sadness anger

diagnoses the unknown sleepless nights fear

accommodations hard conversations waiting hope

problem solving grief advocacy

healing love

This is foster care.

6

Home Operations

TL;DR: It's worth your time to create organized systems in your home for paperwork and scheduling. Get all members of the home collaborating on rules and guidelines so everyone is aligned and expectations are clear.

Set Up for System Success

If you peek inside a typical family's home, you may find a calendar full of sports practices, tutoring, or music lessons. Parents may be working full-time and then coming home to chores, making dinner, and helping with homework. For foster families, there are the typical activities, plus they are co-parenting with the government and the child's parent(s). I call this Group Parenting—and it's hard! There's oversight, policies, procedures, and added responsibilities on top of the typical parenting functions. Having organized and well-maintained paperwork, schedules, and appointments can not only help everyone in the home feel more at ease; it can also help you handle surprises that come your way. Let's break down each piece individually to help you get your home operations as organized as possible from the beginning.

Paperwork

Getting and staying organized with your paperwork is more important than you may realize:

- Submitting monthly paperwork is a foster parent's responsibility.
- Having records and documentation will help you advocate for the child and their needs.
- Keeping track of what is happening in your home creates a record that can help protect you against a false child abuse allegation.

Starting point for setting up a paperwork system:

- Get a list of all monthly forms. Ask if the documents need to be submitted in person or if you can email them.
- Figure out who in the home will be responsible for each form.
- Ask for a digital copy of the forms so you can print them at home, if needed.
- Make sure you have a scan of all documents you turn in for your records.
- Keep copies organized digitally or with a binder system, depending on your personal style. The key is you want to be able to find a document quickly if you need to reference it during a meeting.

Documenting Injuries

Most workers want to be notified of injuries that result in cuts or bruises, especially to the face or head. Typically, they want to see a photo too.

- Make sure you understand your county's reporting requirements and responsibilities (how to report, how quickly, who to contact).

- Ask the worker how they wish to be informed (phone, text, email, or form) and about what type of injuries.
- You are a mandated reporter, so if the injury was caused by another person, you have to disclose who it was and what happened. This may require a hotline report in addition to injury reporting.
- Consider modifying your home to reduce the likelihood of getting hurt.
- If the child gets hurt at daycare/school, make sure you get a written notice detailing what happened from the daycare/school. If they refuse to give this to you, email them a summary of what they told you over the phone or in person so there is a written record.
- If the child is continuously falling down, reach out to their pediatrician for a possible referral. It could be that the child has gross motor or vision needs, for example.
- Make sure you have safety gear that is sized properly for the child for swimming, riding bikes, using their scooter, etc.

Behavior Tracking

For some children, it can be important to track their behavioral or emotional needs. This can be especially important for determining the level of care they need, possible therapeutic interventions, understanding how medication is supportive, or making decisions about which interventions are appropriate. When keeping track of specific behavioral or emotional escalations, you may want to use a calendar or a journal. Consider keeping track of:

- Day of the week
- Time of day

- Duration
- Intensity
- Possible trigger
- What helped them (and what didn't help them)
- Anything else about the day that might be relevant (like missed visit, toilet accident, sub at school)

Lifebook

Keeping milestones, schoolwork, and photos organized in a scrapbook, lifebook, or photo album is an important job for foster parents. When kids move in and out of foster care, you don't want those memories to be lost. I recommend updating it monthly. If you are stumped on what to include each month, these ideas might help:

Photos:

- Celebrating spirit days at school
- Of the child in their spaces: their room, the playroom, their desk, outdoor play area, cooking in the kitchen, etc.
- With their teacher, daycare providers, classmates
- Around town, even running errands, and other everyday moments
- With pets
- At the local park
- Participating in a sport or hobby they love
- Of your extended family who have met the child (and include their names)
- Celebrating their birthday

Written entries:

- Include a funny quote from them, or a silly story or joke they like to tell
- Conduct an interview, and write down the questions and their answers
- Draw their family tree
- Write them a letter to read when they are older (you can also have your permanent kids write a letter)
- Work together to write a plan for a business they want to start
- List the full names of everyone on their professional team
- Make lists of their favorite things
- Write the lyrics to their favorite song
- Write the recipe of their favorite meal
- Make a list of their goals to reach in one year, five years, and ten years
- Write the list of schools they want to attend or companies they want to work for

Projects:

- Schoolwork that demonstrates a new learning milestone or a new skill
- Take a page from their favorite coloring book and have them decorate it
- Trace their handprints and footprints

Keep a flash drive with all of the photos and scans of the written pages so that the youth can have a digital backup!

Family Agreements and House Rules

Posting a written family agreement or list of house rules can be beneficial in your foster home, and for some, it's required by the department. It's a way to align on expectations and consequences for everyone in the home.

Collaboration is an important factor as you develop this agreement. You can start by asking the youth the types of rules that are important to them and what rules help them feel comfortable, respected, and safe in a home. It's important to include what matters to them in addition to what matters to you, so that everyone can feel heard and valued. It's important that all kids and adults follow the family agreement.

Topics/areas to discuss as a family:

- In-home safety (for people and items)
- Substance use, smoking, or vaping
- Friends in the home or visiting friends
- School and homework
- Electronics
- Bathing and personal hygiene
- Cleaning up or household chores
- Privacy
- Home organization
- Pets

As you craft the rules:

- Share. 💬 "The rules are here to keep everyone safe." Explain how individual rules relate to a baseline goal of safety.
- You may need to wait a few weeks before fleshing out the rules, as the kid's needs may change as they settle into the home.
- As part of your discussion, let everyone know that guidelines can be adjusted if they aren't working for everyone.

- You can also discuss consequences as you work through the rules with the family. Natural and logical consequences can be supportive in understanding and learning (see below for more).
- You may want to provide a list of the agreed-upon guidelines to the child's worker to ensure that they are aligned as well.
- Consider posting the agreement where everyone can refer to it. Include icons to enhance understanding.

While it's great to have agreed-upon household guidelines, it's important for you to remember that there will be good and bad days, ups and downs. As kids go through the changes and surprises of foster care, you may notice that it's hard for them to adhere to all of the guidelines. Be open to adjusting or offering redos.

> Let the child know that you're in this together and that you're here to help. For example, "If you have something in your bedroom that is against the rules, or if a friend gave you something to hold for them that is not allowed in this home, you can bring it to me. I will help you figure out what to do with it." Or "If you break a rule, I'd rather you tell me about it than try to hide it or fix it yourself. I can help you. We can figure things out together."

A note about consequences: Traditional parenting methods typically include consequences to teach appropriate behavioral responses. Within a foster home, some punitive consequences can harm trust or bonds, or could cause kids to feel shame or fear. It is important to not take this personally and to understand that their brains have been wired for survival. Because of this, in many foster homes, *finding teachable moments* may be better suited. When a child breaks a rule, regrouping when they are calm about what happened and what could be done differently can help build new skills. Acknowledging or praising them when they demonstrate these skills in the future can be a way to encourage them to continue to use healthier coping skills.

Sometimes enforcing a boundary is needed to keep kids safe, and a related consequence can help in this moment.

For example, if two kids are starting to hit and push each other, enforcing a boundary would be you stepping in between the children to separate them.

A related consequence is that playtime is over and the kids have to play separately.

After both have calmed down, you can all talk about how to solve problems better in the future.

You, as the foster parent, may also need to provide closer supervision until they have learned this skill to ensure safety. Your closer supervision can help remind them of the agreed-upon ways to solve problems in the moment.

A punitive unrelated consequence would be not allowing candy for dessert because they were hitting. While this may work for some, if this is a new relationship with a child, it can cause more dysregulation or could cause the child to sneak or hide candy. They may be less likely to tell you they were hit by their sibling in the future.

There may be times when each kid will have different rules or consequences, especially if you have permanent children in your home too. "Each kid in this home gets what they need, and it may not always be the same thing." "You each need something different to help you grow and learn." "The goal isn't for everyone to get the same thing; instead, our goal is to make sure each kid feels supported and safe. What do you need right now to feel safe and supported?"

Scheduling and Appointments

The first month will have a flurry of appointments, but after the initial set of meetings, things should settle into a routine. You may have parent visits, worker visits, advocate visits, kids therapy sessions, and extracurricular activities. And don't forget to build in that weekly one-on-one time with your permanent children too!

If you're feeling overwhelmed by all of the appointments:

- **Use a shared calendar** with your partner and the older youth in the home (if it's appropriate). That way everyone can be on the same page. Some people like to post a whiteboard-style calendar somewhere everyone in the home can see, while others prefer a digital calendar.

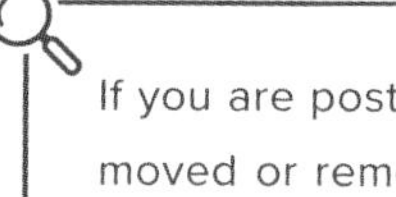

> If you are posting a calendar, you may want one that can be moved or removed when company is over to visit. You may not want friends or extended family to see specific appointments that the child wishes to keep private.

- **Schedule ahead** whenever possible. By asking the worker if you can get next month's appointment on the calendar, you may be able to select a day and time that's most convenient for your family.
- **Ask for support,** such as transportation support for visits or school. In some situations, foster parents are asked to monitor the parent visits. You could ask the worker to find someone to supervise the visits instead of you.

- **Double-book** whenever possible. Sometimes the agency worker can visit at the same time as the county worker, for example. By doubling up these appointments, you can save some time!
- **Ask about flexibility** with appointments. For example, are virtual appointments a possibility? Is the child required to attend or just the foster parent? More flexibility will make your life easier.
- **Hold at least one day during the week when you don't book any meetings** related to foster care. This gives everyone in the home a break!
- **Plan ahead for school breaks or holidays.** These times can get tricky, and sometimes visits have to be moved around to accommodate days off. Plan ahead for adjustments so you can be sure you get a day and time that is convenient for your family.
- **Call a team meeting** if you find that the schedule is overwhelming for you or the child. Sometimes these appointments start getting stacked up, and when you take a step back and look at it all, you realize how unsustainable it is. Get the worker involved in figuring out a new schedule that works better for everyone.

Your future self will thank you for having been proactive about schedules, paperwork, and home expectations. Foster care comes with shifts and surprises. When you have everything organized at home, you can move through these changes more easily.

7
Foundational Trauma-Conscious Skills

TL;DR: Being a trauma-conscious parent requires you to meet kids where they are at and show up in the hardest moments in a purposeful way. With predictability, tolerance, connection, curiosity, regulation support, and the ability to think on your feet, you can offer steady support through the ups and downs of foster care.

Trauma-Conscious Parenting

Big emotions, such as feelings of anger, sadness, and worry, are common for all kids, and it's the parent's job to help them learn coping skills so they can move through these moments safely. You'll see moments of dysregulation in foster homes, too, but often with higher frequency, duration, and intensity, or they're triggered by something related to a past experience, like physical abuse, neglect, or witnessing domestic violence. Kids' minds and bodies may react to being triggered in ways that they can't control. A time-out or taking away a privilege won't make these responses stop. They require therapeutic interventions from foster parents and professionals.

WHAT THIS MIGHT LOOK LIKE IN A FOSTER HOME (BY AGE):		
Infants	Stiff body Avoiding eye contact Shaking / Easily startled Not crying or crying too much Not showing emotions Not eating enough	Digestion problems Irritable / Difficult to soothe Not hitting developmental milestones
Younger Child	Startles easily or hides Sleep trouble, nightmares Physical complaints Clinginess Scared to be alone, fearful Low frustration tolerance Low self-confidence Difficult to soothe Reenacting trauma through play Loss of skills or developmental delays	Overeating or loss of appetite Bathroom accidents, bed-wetting Flat affect Uninterested in play Destructive or aggressive Forgetful or making up stories Easily distracted Inconsolable screaming or crying Shame or guilt Taking things, hiding objects
Older Youth	Anxious, scared Avoidant of places Bed-wetting Sleep trouble or excessive sleepiness Flashbacks Dissociation Destructive or aggressive behaviors Regressing to childlike behaviors Shame or guilt Overeating or loss of appetite Withdrawn, isolated School refusal	Change in friend groups or relationships Forgetfulness, memory or concentration concerns Lying or avoiding the truth Substance use Leaving the home/ running away Depressed Self-harm Sabotaging big days or events Pushing away caregivers Constantly seeking approval of adults

Supporting trauma responses and emotional needs is at the core of foster parenting.

I want to start by sharing some foundational parenting skills that can help you as you navigate the nuances of parenting kids who've experienced trauma. These are things that I do in my home on a day-to-day basis, and they have come up over and over again in community feedback. You'll see these themes repeated throughout this entire book. When I asked my audience, "What are 'foster parenting basics'?" these are the six core skills that were shared.

The six foundational parenting skills (according to the community):

1. Predictability
2. Tolerance
3. Connection
4. Curiosity
5. Regulation support
6. Ability to think on your feet

When a child moves in, they are a stranger, and you don't know yet what they will need. Think of this as a starting point for you to learn about them, help them through hard moments, establish trust, and form a bond. The end goal is for you to understand them well enough that you can anticipate their trauma-related needs and help them learn positive coping skills.

Predictability

Predictability can help kids feel safe and secure in your home, reduce anxious feelings, and learn to trust you.

What this can look like:

- Foreshadowing with words, play, printed visuals, or videos of what is going to happen or what the kid can expect next
- Having a consistently stocked fridge
- Showing up on time
- Serving safe food/packaged food (that tastes the same every time!)
- Reliable routines for meals, morning, bedtime, and visits
- Having consistently calm reactions during stressful situations
- Keeping your promises to demonstrate that you can be counted on during times of need

Over time, you will gain a greater understanding of their needs and likely won't have to provide so many points of predictability during the day. Youth will also start to feel more secure and trusting in your caregiving, so they will be able to naturally feel more at ease when things come up—like if you are a few minutes late picking them up or if the fridge gets a little empty at the end of the week. Since they know you are reliable, they likely will be less reactive to these types of things. You can also help them use tools themselves, like a whiteboard calendar in their room, to help them create predictability for themselves.

Tolerance

Tolerance is all about the foster parent expanding their levels of tolerance, challenging their parenting beliefs, and being open to a different way of engaging with and supporting kids.

What this can look like:

- Modifying your house rules to be more developmentally appropriate for the child

- Choosing your battles, such as tolerating cursing to express anger as a replacement for being physically aggressive (it's a step in a safer direction!)
- Giving kids choice and control in everyday moments, like choosing what they eat or what show gets put on the TV
- Accepting kids as they are today, including regressions and their desires to use things that are usually for younger children
- Being open to repeating requests, directions, and reminders without punishment or shame
- Modifying your home to be better set up for the sensory and safety needs of the youth
- Incorporating and celebrating the child's cultural and religious needs and traditions so that they don't feel excluded
- Having an open mind about different discipline or parenting practices that best match the child's needs, or being open to compromising on plans or consequences.
- Adapting your communication style to the youth's style (e.g., journal, text, talking in the car).
- Understanding that sometimes it is better to be *safe* than *right*. Arguments about who is right or wrong can lead to unsafe escalations. If you notice this might happen, it can be better to pause the conversation and revisit it later or possibly let it go completely.
- Accepting that this kind of parenting may not look or feel like what you had imagined before you started fostering.

Over time, as you learn different parenting techniques from the various professionals you work with, you will find certain discipline and teaching strategies to be more effective for each child. The child will respond better to your guidance when they feel valued and affirmed. When youth become more comfortable in your home and their life has settled down into more of a rhythm, you can start to teach new skills to help them reach new developmental levels.

Connection

Connection points throughout the day can help not just with bonding and attachment, but also with regulation and de-escalation throughout the day.

What this can look like:

- Leaving a note in their lunch box
- Exchanging a journal
- Physical closeness, like sitting together or nearby
- Rocking and singing to them
- Taking a walk or hike together
- Going for a drive together
- Offering a hug
- Taking an interest in their interests
- Cooking/baking together
- Giving a baby or toddler a bath
- Responsiveness to their needs
- Reading a book together
- Active listening
- Lighting up and showing joy when they enter the room
- Loving them just as they are

- Owning mistakes and repairing: 💬 "I should have walked away and taken a deep breath." "I should not have raised my voice." "I am the grown-up, and it is my job to remain calm." "I want to tell you something important. Yesterday I messed up. That was not okay, and I shouldn't have done it." "That was my mistake."

Over time, the nurturing you have consistently provided will help the child feel comfortable coming to you about the hard stuff when they need advice or help. This solid connection can help carry them through the hardest moments in foster care. Even if you don't have a relationship after reunification, you will have shown them that adults can be trusted and can help them feel better. You're building a foundation for connection that they will carry into the future.

Curiosity

Curiosity gives foster parents a chance to better understand the child's needs. It can also help with emotional regulation and avoiding an escalation. Your curiosity needs to be genuine and free from judgment or criticism. Kids who've experienced trauma often can sense when adults are being disingenuous.

What this can look like:

- Open body language, supportive facial expressions (rather than angry or closed off)
- Curious lines of questioning: 💬 "Help me understand..." "How can I better support you?" "Can you explain it to me in a different way?" "I'm noticing some signs that you are feeling something right now. I'm not sure what's going on..."

- Using a printed collage of photos of items or situations that can help kids feel better (such as blowing bubbles, cuddling a lovey, or reading a book). Then ask, 💬 "What do you need right now?"
- For kids who struggle with open-ended questions, saying something like, 💬 "I am wondering if you are feeling upset that your mom missed the visit." It may be easier for kids to nod or use a simple yes or no.
- For little ones, incorporating into play a scenario that you want to understand better. Pretend a toy or stuffed animal is a baby crying, and then ask the child, 💬 "How do we help Baby?" Their suggestions may be an indication of what they need in similar moments too.
- For kids who have a hard time sharing their own feelings and needs, using photos of children showing different emotions, and asking, 💬 "Why do you think they are so sad?" or "What is this kid thinking about?" What the child says may be a reflection of their own true thoughts and feelings.
- For older youth, who may seem like they are trying to manipulate certain situations or be defiant, remembering that there is always an unmet need or an underdeveloped skill underneath these behaviors. I've heard Dr. Becky Kennedy share this sentiment, and it rings true in the foster care world, as well: They aren't trying to *give you* a hard time; they are *having* a hard time. Sometimes they won't tell you directly what's going on, so you have to piece things together in other ways.

Over time, youth will feel valued and heard, which opens up so many more conversations and opportunities for foster parents to guide and teach. You can also help them better understand themselves and what they need when they are feeling upset or out of control. These are valuable skills they will take into adulthood.

Regulation Support

Regulation support is a powerful tool to help kids stay safe throughout the day during behavioral and emotional highs and lows, or when triggered by a situation related to their trauma. Activities that can help keep kids' bodies regulated throughout the day can reduce escalations.

What this can look like:

- Using a calm, neutral tone, and make sure your body language is also calm (arms, legs, face, stance, breathing)
- Demonstrating taking a deep breath
- Offering sensory supports, such as a weighted blanket, noise-canceling headphones, fidget toys, or chewelry (wearable items that are safe for kids to chew or bite)
- Physical activity through walks, exercise, or involvement in sports
- Offering gentle words of support: 💬 "I'm here." "You're safe."
- Building in time for rest, extra naps, or mental health days
- Encouraging creative expression such as journaling, music, or art
- Engaging their different senses:
  - » Sight: playing I spy
  - » Hearing: going outside and seeing if you can identify the neighborhood sounds
  - » Smell: smelling a candle and trying to guess the scent
  - » Touch: asking them to find treasures you hide in Thinking Putty (like beads or jewels)

» Taste: offering an ice-cold water, Popsicle, or sour candy
» Doing a visualization exercise together: "If you could be anywhere right now, where would you be?" Ask them to describe the scene using all five senses.

If you—the foster parent—are triggered and dysregulated, you will not be able to coregulate (support their nervous system with your calm presence). While you work on finding *your* calm, you'll need to think on your feet (details below) and apply a bit of a parenting Band-Aid while you take a moment to regulate yourself.

A FOSTER PARENT IN THE COMMUNITY SHARED

"One thing that helped is that I developed mindfulness skills. Being better prepared to stay focused on the present moment has been so helpful in staying focused on loving children amidst all the chaos."

Other ideas to help find *your* calm in the moment can be sipping ice-cold water, breathing or grounding exercises, splashing some water on your face, or turning on calming music.

Over time, youth will start to learn about the types of things that help them feel better. You can go from coregulating to reminding them about their coping skills, to watching them access these skills independently. Once they understand what they need to feel better, they will be able to more safely endure all the ups and downs that come with foster care and beyond.

Ability to Think on Your Feet

The ability to think on your feet can get you and the child out of many tricky moments. This is all about distractions, redirections, and gamifying requests that are hard for kids. While all feelings are valid and should be honored, the expression of those feelings may not always be safe depending on where you are and what else is going on. The key is to try to redirect the child to something else before a full escalation occurs. Even if the child is escalated, sometimes these things will help get you a moment of calm so you can move them to a safer place (such as getting out of a store and into the car).

What this can look like:

- Moving to a new location to change the vibe—like going outside or going to a different room in the home
- Putting on a calming or meditation video on your phone (you can find many for free on YouTube)
- For younger kids, a silly or gamified transition: 💬 "How many steps will it take to get to the door? I think twenty!" or "Let's walk like robots. First, let me program you. Beep boop beep!"
- Distracting or redirecting the child by putting on a TV show, offering them a new activity or toy to play with, or making a strange request, like, 💬 "I'm not sure I cleaned out the lint filter. Let's go check!" Suddenly they may be less mad that they can't play with a toy and

more excited to experience that satisfying feeling of cleaning out a lint trap!

- Using a "calming box" (a small box filled with fidgets, a sketch pad, sensory items, etc.) to help pass time—like in a waiting room or at a long team meeting
- For older youth, stalling tactics like, "I was planning on ordering some food. Before you leave, do you want to hang out for a little bit and at least eat? Let's put on a movie while we wait for it to be delivered," or "Why don't you finish your show, and I'll be back in twenty minutes?" Drawing things out can give youth time to regulate, and they may be less likely to do something dangerous or impulsive (like leave the home).
- Negotiating with the youth on what the plan is or what will happen next. Giving them power or finding a way for them to "win" can help de-escalate.

> It's important to note that you shouldn't always redirect or distract a child from feeling their feelings. You don't want them to feel like you are dismissing how they feel. Some kids may have been told it wasn't okay to cry or that their feelings were "too much" for their parent(s). Make sure you are using redirections and distractions with purpose. A mental health professional can help you figure out how to best support the youth in various situations.

Over time, these quick interventions will become less frequently needed or may be something that is only needed during the hardest moments in the day (like getting into bed!). As kids work through their trauma with a professional, you may find that they need these types of interventions less frequently.

Kids don't need perfect foster parents. If you strive for perfection, you will fail. We all make mistakes. This book is made possible by the thousands of people who have messed up and learned a better way to do things. Acknowledging, apologizing, and repairing are just as important as getting it "right" as you move through your own learnings.

8

Trauma Responses, Big Feelings, and Dysregulation

TL;DR: A child may be triggered by common daily life occurrences because of abuse or neglect they experienced. Providing accommodations or preparing youth for these occurrences can help them in the moment. Children may have a variety of valid emotions. Foster parents can help them find healthy coping skills and safe ways to process through connection, comfort, accommodations, and creative and physical outlets.

In addition to having foundational trauma-conscious parenting skills from the previous chapter, it's important to understand nuances related to specific trauma-related experiences.

Trauma Responses

As a foster parent, it's really important you understand how the brain is affected by trauma. It changes the way that kids perceive the world around them, and respond to everyday moments and stressors. This understanding will help you see these behaviors and emotional responses differently and with more compassion.

The National Child Traumatic Stress Network describes the impact of trauma on children this way:

> Traumatic experiences can initiate strong emotions and physical reactions that can persist long after the event… Children who suffer from traumatic stress often have these types of symptoms when reminded in some way of the traumatic event. Although many of us may experience reactions to stress from time to time, when a child is experiencing traumatic stress, these reactions interfere with the child's daily life and ability to function and interact with others.[1]

All kids who are in foster care have experienced trauma. Trauma responses can cause kids to feel, speak, or behave in certain ways that may look like they are misbehaving or are being defiant. This isn't in their control. It takes time for kids to work through and heal from their trauma. You have to trust that the healing is happening and that the steps you take to help them will have an impact. Foster parents may never see a child heal from these traumatic experiences, since they may only be in their home for a short amount of time. The good news is that there is so much you can do to create a supportive environment and help them cope and move through these hard moments.

The following traumas are common experiences for youth in foster care, and it's easy for them to be reminded (consciously or subconsciously) of these traumas by everyday events or circumstances that wouldn't normally faze those who haven't experienced them. While these aren't

1 "About Child Trauma," The National Child Traumatic Stress Network, accessed July 16, 2025, https://www.nctsn.org/what-is-child-trauma/about-child-trauma.

exhaustive lists, they are crowdsourced from thousands of comments to give you as much context as possible in these scenarios.

System Trauma/Removal from Home

Things that may be triggering or difficult for the children in your care:

- People of authority and their vehicles: police cars, helicopters, white vans/department vehicles, fire trucks, ambulances, sirens
- Workers visiting the home, surprise visits at the home, the doorbell ringing
- Saying goodbye to friends, family, or siblings
- Adults going through the youth's personal belongings or bedroom
- Car rides, not telling kids where they are going
- Parent visits
- Court, attorneys, judges
- Being woken up unexpectedly or harshly
- Getting pulled out of class or being asked to go to the office

What you can do to help:

- Ask people to text when they arrive instead of ringing the doorbell
- Let the child know why people are visiting the home
- Explain a situation as it's happening (💬 "That's a police siren. You are safe. They aren't coming here.")
- Don't threaten to disrupt (✖ "If you run away again, I'm going to have to tell the worker I can't foster you anymore.")
- Reiterate to the youth that they aren't leaving your home when the worker visits (double-check with the worker before you promise this)

- Explain their needs and possible triggers to school staff
- Loop the worker into specific concerns, as they may have creative ways to work around the triggers related to the foster care system

History of Witnessing or Experiencing Abuse (Domestic, Physical, Verbal)

Things that may be triggering or difficult:

- People of authority and their vehicles: Police cars, helicopters, white vans/department vehicles, fire trucks, ambulances, sirens
- Being cornered, being blocked from an exit, standing in doorways
- Someone taking off a belt or taking off shoes
- Specific holidays or anniversaries—especially if they are related to celebrating a person or a relationship
- The sound of a can or bottle opening, alcohol consumption
- Specific scents like aftershave, perfume, cigarette smoke
- Raised voices, yelling, loud noises
- Adults arguing or having a disagreement within earshot
- A baby or their sibling crying—especially when out of their eyesight
- Sudden movements toward the child
- School calling home to report a problem with the child
- Partners being affectionate with each other
- Dropping, spilling, or breaking something by accident
- Getting in trouble at home
- Someone pushing their head underwater (during a bath or at a pool), or pushing them into a pool

What you can do to help:

- Maintain composure when treating wounds from the abuse—try not to make the child feel bad about what happened (✖ "Oh my god! I can't believe what happened to you! This is horrible!" This may be interpreted by the child as if they did something wrong.)
- Move slowly and quietly around the home. Don't play loud or violent movies after they go to bed. They could misinterpret these noises as something actually happening in the home.
- Keep a calm voice and body language during disagreements; keep hands down (try not to talk with your hands)
- Explain situations that could be triggering as they happen. 💬 "Baby brother is crying, but he is okay and safe. I will rock him and feed him to help him feel better. I don't get upset when he cries; I am here to help him."
- Reiterate how your family responds to problems. 💬 "In this home, we don't hurt other people with our words or our bodies." "When kids or adults make a mistake, we talk about it and help each other. We don't yell or hit someone if they mess up."
- Keep disagreements between you and your partner private and away from the children
- Drink responsibly or avoid alcohol altogether
- Work with a therapist to help you form a trusting relationship with the youth

History of Sexual Abuse

Things that may be triggering or difficult:

- Bathrooms, bathtubs, bath time

- Comments or excessive compliments about their appearance
- Diaper changes
- Going to the dentist, having teeth worked on
- Entering their bedroom without permission, checking on them in the middle of the night without them calling out first
- Being in the complete dark, forcing them to close their eyes at bedtime
- Being cornered, being blocked from an exit, standing in doorways
- Specific scents like aftershave or perfume
- Tickling, roughhousing
- Not seeing hands above tables or blankets, sharing a blanket
- Light touch, startling touch
- Church, youth groups, overnight camps
- Sleepovers, strangers sleeping over in the home
- Receiving expensive gifts
- Being required to hug people or sit on laps
- Secrets or saying things like, ✖ "I'm going to tell you a secret"

What you can do to help:

- Respect their personal space and bodies
- Ask for consent before entering their room, physical interactions, or taking their photo
- Avoid the use of certain scents
- Accept and support which foster parent the youth prefers
- Allow them an out if they want to leave a place quickly or early (you can use a code word, signal, or emoji)
- Request female professionals at the doctor, dentist, etc.

- Provide plenty of options for light in their bedroom so they can layer or dim them as needed
- Explain what to expect for forensic exams (see more about this below), investigations, or other triggering appointments (like medical or dental appointments)
- Respect their needs and boundaries, and acknowledge that it's healthy and welcome to have boundaries. 💬 "Your needs are not a burden." "You're not asking too much." "Thank you for setting a boundary. I respect your boundary." "You are in charge of your own body, and I'm in charge of my body. Everyone is in charge of their own bodies."
- Enter into conversations with empathy. 💬 "How can I best support you?" "Is it okay if I talk to you more about this?"
- Connect them with a professional or share supportive hotlines/text lines and resources in the home.

Details about a forensic exam: A forensic exam typically happens when there's concerns about sexual abuse, but it can also include physical abuse or neglect. This is a specialized medical appointment that is used for treatment and investigations. At times, the worker may handle this appointment entirely with the youth or this appointment may happen before the child arrives at your home. The appointment can be very triggering, so if you are taking the child, *know this before you go*:

- If the abuse happened recently, you'll need to follow necessary steps from their worker, department, and medical professionals. Often it is requested that the youth not bathe before being examined, so ask about this.
- If the appointment is scheduled in advance, call ahead and get all of the info you can. The whole day will be less stressful if you're clear on

all the logistics: parking, finding the office, checking in, etc. By knowing what to expect, you can focus your attention on being calm and supportive to the youth.

- There may be a urine test during the appointment, so bring a preferred drink, like juice. If the child is in a diaper or pull-up, the medical professional can put something in the diaper to catch the urine. Having lots of liquids available can help speed this process up and make it a little easier for the child.
- The professionals may prefer to do all of the talking and prepping, or it may be up to you to prepare the youth for the appointment. For example, it may be helpful to share: 💬 "The doctor will look at all of your body parts and ask questions about your body," "The doctor may need to take photos or videos of your body," or "You may be asked some questions about what you've been going through."
- If you are interviewed, know that this is not necessarily confidential. Your responses may be shared with the medical team and the investigator. It may make sense for you to share away from where the child can hear you. You may be asked about their behaviors, such as bed-wetting, bathing, changing, etc., and those sensitive topics are hard for some kids to hear about. You don't want them to feel bad about the things they are doing, as it isn't their fault. But without maturity and context, kids may misunderstand what is being said.

A quick note if there is a fear of men: Some youth may have unique fears of men due to their trauma history. If you are a foster dad, you may need to go above and beyond to help youth feel comfortable with you in the home. Try not to take it personally if the youth does not want to be near you or is scared to be around you at first. It may take you longer to earn their trust.

History of Neglect

Things that may be triggering or difficult:

- Control of food (✖ "No snacks 'til dinner." "No candy allowed in this house.")
- Lack of food, running out of food, empty fridge
- Hot cars or being left in the car
- Sick caregiver or parent
- Smoking, vaping, pill bottles, alcohol use
- Wearing dirty diapers or clothing for long periods of time
- Making jokes or expressing real concerns about money, food, or employment in front of the child
- Staying in hotels or camping in tents
- Receiving expensive gifts
- Time-outs or being sent to their room alone
- Leaving kids with babysitters
- Showing up late to daycare or school pickup
- Not being in eyesight of foster parent (they may want to be next to you all of the time)

What you can do to help:

- Ask about therapeutic baby massages, or learn how to do them yourself (there are videos on YouTube).

- Check on babies at night, even if they aren't crying, and follow their doctor's recommendation about feeding at night.
- Change bedding, clothing, and diapers as soon as they become soiled
- Be direct about being able to meet their needs or the needs of siblings. "We will always have food to eat." "Even though I have a cold and I'm not feeling my best, I am still able to get you dinner." "Your baby sister is crying, so I'm going to get her what she needs—a bottle and a fresh diaper."
- Drink responsibly, or avoid alcohol altogether.
- Find discipline strategies that *don't* require the child to be left alone in their room. For example, a "time-in" may be more effective, where you join them in a safe space to coregulate.
- Explain to them where you are going and when you will be home.

If you are going to arrive home after they have gone to bed, you can figure out a system where you check on them at night and leave them a note or a stuffy so they know you came home.

- Allow them to open your bedroom door at night to make sure that you are home.
- Keep conversations about concerns about money or job loss private and out of earshot.
- Call ahead to the daycare or school if you know you will be late for pickup to assure the child you are coming.
- Never leave young kids in the car, even for a short amount of time. (This may be triggering and can also be incredibly dangerous. In most states, leaving younger children in the car unattended is illegal.)

- Keep plenty of food on hand at all times. (See chapter 11 for more information about hoarding/hiding food.)

A quick note about caring for infants exposed to substances: This is a unique trauma that often requires medical support as the baby experiences withdrawal symptoms. Please consider seeking medical support or training from the baby's medical team. Additionally, there is a class you can take from Foster Parent College that reviews various substances and the different support needs a baby may have.

> Ask your worker if they will cover the cost of Foster Parent College classes!

Parentification

When a child, usually the older one, takes on the parenting role for the adults or children in the home, you can support them by:

- Starting with curiosity and opening the door for them to share. "If you ever want to talk about what that was like for you, I am here to listen." "Can you tell me about your little sibling? What do they like to eat, play with, read? What are their fears? What makes them happy? What do you love about your sibling?"
- Underscoring their important role. "Your love and care for your sibling is so strong. You are such an important person in their life."
- Taking it slow. Instead of putting down firm boundaries, walk alongside the parentified child.

- Observing them and then creating instances where they can observe you or you can gently join in. Find a balance of incorporating their feedback, while also showcasing your parenting skills and knowledge. "I love how you picked him up and sang that song to him. Next time he is crying, I'd like to try to help him." "Next time he needs his diaper changed, I'd like to help. I can do the poopy ones if you'd like!"
- Including them in updates on the child, such as having them join for a doctor's appointment, explaining to them the services they are going to be getting, etc. While it's important foster parents are the decision-makers, shutting the sibling out of what is going on may backfire.
- Offering a choice, when appropriate. Examples could be including them in choosing a theme for the child's birthday party or offering for them to help with bath or bedtime.
- Finding sibling-appropriate care tasks such as helping with homework. This can help them still feel connected without taking on parenting responsibilities.
- Folding in activities for the older sibling to be with peers. Learn their special interests/hobbies, and try to find activities and extracurriculars that reconnect them with kids their age. This can help them feel like a kid again.
- Understanding that this may be a very long road, and sometimes, you may never see a resolution. Sadly, many kids jump around from home to home, so some siblings will never fully drop their role as a parent. They will always feel they need to be there for their sibling in case they return back home or go to a neglectful foster home.
- Requesting therapy for the older sibling, so they can start to work through and process this trauma.

Sometimes siblings are separated, which can cause greater stress for a youth who is used to taking care of their sibling:

- Take their concerns for their siblings seriously. Follow up with the worker and try to find answers to their questions.
- Advocate for sibling visits, including in-person, phone calls, meetups at school, etc. You may need to take the initiative to set these up.
- When visits aren't possible or are limited, encourage writing letters or drawing photos to save for later, creating a memory book together, reading books about missing someone, and always being open to listening to them talk about their sibling.
- Don't forget all of the meaningful sibling relationships, including half, fictive kin (nonrelatives treated like family), and stepsiblings on both sides of the family, as well as adult siblings.

When Kids Have Had to Be a Parent to Their Parent

Some youth had to take care of the adults in their home and may try to take care of the foster parent too. Foster parents can remind them they are safe and that it's their job to be a kid. 💬 "I am responsible for myself and my own feelings. I have Chris and my mom who can take care of me if I'm sick."

You can acknowledge their efforts and intentions to help but also be sure you offer praise when they do something for themselves or choose themselves for a change. 💬 "Thank you for cleaning. I'm curious; is there anything you'd rather be doing than cleaning?" "I noticed that you chose to color and then set up your train display. I'm proud of you for having fun and choosing yourself."

IF A CHILD DISCLOSES ABUSE TO YOU

Kids may disclose to you the abuse they have experienced. It can happen very quickly in your time together (like randomly in the middle of family dinner), or it may come out once they feel safe with you. If this occurs, you can greet this moment with gentleness and compassion. 💬 "That must have been so hard for you." "You are so brave to tell me about what happened." "I am so sorry that happened." "Grown-ups are not allowed to do that." "That will not happen in this home." "I believe you." "Do you want to share anything more?" "Thank you for telling me." Follow department protocols for mandated reporting. See chapter 5 for how you can explain mandated reporting to kids.

Emotional Support Ideas

Sadness/Grief/Depression

Being removed from parents, siblings, community, and loved ones can cause immense feelings of loss and sadness. And unfortunately, for some kids in foster care, they may also experience the death of a parent, sibling, or relative. This emotional response may cause a child to want to hide or be alone, and sometimes it can turn into deeper safety concerns like self-harm or suicidal thoughts.

What you can do to help:

- Acknowledge their feelings and help them put words to them. Grief, loss, and sadness are valid responses to what has happened in their life. 💬 "It's okay to cry." "It's okay to feel more than one thing at a time. You may feel sadness and happiness."

- Create a safe environment for them to feel their feelings. You can offer a communication journal so older youth can share with you things that are hard to talk about. Reiterate your care. "You are brave and smart. There isn't anything you can say that will change how I feel about you."
- Offer opportunities for rest, relaxation, and self-care, such as bath bombs, yoga, coloring, mental health days, etc.
- Gently offer to join them in moments of retreat, like when they are playing video games or isolating in their room.
- Encourage their connections to others, such as a best friend, a favorite aunt, a coach, or connect them with a school counselor.

> If you notice them withdrawing from social situations or activities they love, or a significant increase in time spent alone, this can be a sign of distress. "I've noticed you've been spending more time alone. We all need a break sometimes. Is anything going on? I just want to make sure I'm not missing anything."

- Facilitate interactions with pets or advocate for animal-assisted therapies like equine therapy.
- Find opportunities for them to "escape," such as going to the movies, a concert, or picking out a new chapter book at the library.
- Find opportunities for them to process feelings and express themselves creatively.
- If they share concerning comments (like wishing they were dead), you can ask directly if they have ever thought about harming themselves. They may be glad you brought it up. "Thank you for telling me. You are not alone. I'm here to support you through this. Have you ever thought about harming yourself?"

- Connect them with a therapist or psychiatrist for professional support and to develop a safety plan. Leave brochures or hotline/text line numbers in their bedroom for crisis support, and remind them that if they use them, they can remain anonymous.

Anger/Escalations

Anger and frustration are common, and valid, responses the child may feel about what's happening in their life. The key here is safety. Anger and frustration can escalate into unsafe situations or a crisis, but foster parents can help kids learn healthier and safer coping skills when they are feeling this way.

It's important to remember anger is often a secondary emotion, and when you can get to the root of the problem, you will find fear, sadness, or shame. Kids may express this as anger and start to escalate, and may have little to no control over this reaction. Their brain is in survival mode. Anger can protect a child from feeling exposed or vulnerable. When you see anger, safety comes first, and then comes repair, connection, and understanding.

What you can do to help:

- Offer plenty of full-body gross-motor activities and outlets. This can include exercise equipment and classes, punching bags, sports activities, crash pads, and play structures.
- Let them vent without judgment. Validate their frustrations and anger. 💬 "It makes sense that you are mad." "It's good to vent about stuff. I'm always here to listen." "I hear you; your feelings are valid." Or repeat back to them what they have shared.

- Demonstrate in real time how to handle anger in a real situation, or role-play a situation in which someone is angry. "I'm feeling really angry right now about this email I just received. I gotta go for a walk around the block. Anyone want to join?" For younger kids, you can use toys for role-playing.
- Offer ways to express anger through emotional music, bold art projects, or a diary for journaling or angry writing.
- Advocate for therapy or, if needed, intensive home-based services, if you have concerns about their safety or the safety of others in the home.
- Develop a safety or crisis plan with the professional team. During an escalation, refer to this plan.
- Debrief after an escalation. Work with them to find different ways to express feelings that are safer for themselves and others at home. Understand that some youth may not be able to remember everything clearly. *Remember that sometimes it's better to be safe than right.*
- Repair together. "People are more important than things." "Everything has a solution." "We're on the same team." Welcome their efforts to fix something that's broken or to write an apology letter. This can help them feel better about themselves.

> If property has been damaged, you may be able to submit a claim with the department for reimbursement. Each department has different rules as to what and how they reimburse, so ask your worker for details.

Tools for Emotional Support and Expression

- ☐ **Creative outlets:** art supplies, musical instruments, music player, journal or diary with colorful pens or highlighters, dance classes, or chalk to express their feelings in a creative way
- ☐ **Physical activity:** yoga mat, outdoor playset, jump rope, punching bag, bike, or scooter can help release pent-up anger or frustration
- ☐ **Regulation:** crash pads, chewing gum, sour candy, swings, sensory socks, bubbles, thinking putty, chewelry to help kids regulate and process
- ☐ **Comfort:** a soft blanket, stuffed animal, loveys, fuzzy socks, tents, tunnels, mats, or blankets for burrowing can also help provide comfort
- ☐ **Books about topics that mirror the child's experiences and feelings:** When a child sees themselves in a book, it can help them feel seen, and it can help open the door to conversations. From grief to anger, there's usually a kids book for it!

I WANT TO PASS ALONG THIS IMPORTANT REMINDER FROM A FELLOW FOSTER PARENT

"Most of the 'behaviors' of kids have absolutely nothing to do with you. It hurts in the moment, but try to hold on to the fact that they're working through feelings from trauma and not passing judgment on you as a person. You're just the safest target they've found."

9

Elevated Behavioral Needs

TL;DR: Lying, fear of being alone, taking things, and running away can be "typical kid" behaviors, but for children with a history of trauma, these behaviors tend to be more intense, as they are based in fear, unmet needs, and survival instincts. Using foundational trauma-conscious skills, foster parents can help kids find better ways to cope and get their needs met.

Intensive Support Needs in a Foster Home

It's developmentally appropriate and typical for kids to test boundaries and break rules. Part of growing up is messing up and having parents step in to teach them better ways to address their needs. In foster homes, this may look and feel different due to the youth's trauma background. You may see elevated needs that are more risky or require professional support. In this chapter, you'll learn about some of the most common behavioral needs. Remember the six skills discussed in chapter 7; you'll see these themes play out in the tips and considerations below. I've included some of the most common behaviors in this section that my community members have shared.

Lying/Avoiding the Truth

Not telling the truth is a common trauma response for kids in foster care. For them, lying or avoiding the truth may have been a *survival* technique. Maybe they had to lie or their parent(s) asked them to lie, and they felt they had to, or they would get in trouble (or possibly even abused). Kids also lie to foster parents because they are unsure how you will respond and whether it's safe to tell the truth.

What you can do to help:

- Avoid asking directly about something you already know the answer to or can easily discover the answer to. Instead of ✕ "Did you brush your teeth?" go in and check if the toothbrush is wet so you already know the answer. This can be applied to a lot of situations.
- Listen to their side of the story. For example, if the school calls and says something happened, while you can get some truth from that call, there will always be more info from the child. Showing the child you are listening to their side can help build trust.
- Offer a variety of ways for kids to communicate hard things. They can write you a note in a shared journal, explain what happened to a preferred parent or to their therapist (rather than you), or they can *show* you (rather than tell you) through play or pointing.
- Offer help in telling the truth. "Do you want to share what happened, or do you want me to guess, and you can tell me if I'm right?" This small change can help kids be more truthful when you are saying the words and they only have to say yes or no. Your tone will be important here: soft, caring, nurturing, kind.
- Role-play truth-telling. Sometimes my husband and I would role-play a tough situation where one of us tells the truth and the other

person receives hard news. This can show kids how these instances are handled in the home and can give them more confidence to tell the truth during harder situations.

- Reiterate there is no punishment and you won't yell at them. Of course, there may be consequences beyond your control (for example, using AI on an assignment may lead to disciplinary measures at school). 💬 "Remember, I will not get angry, no matter what you tell me. I won't yell or hit you. We will still have dinner, and I will still tuck you in at night."
- Tolerate more in the moment. If the lie is not harming anything, sometimes it is not worth the argument and harming your connection with the child. You can always revisit the situation later after the heat of the moment. 💬 "Okay, thank you for explaining what happened." You can move on from the conversation and then spend some time thinking about what you can change to help them feel safer and more likely to tell the truth next time. We won't always get it right, and kids also need time to trust us and feel safe.
- Offer a redo for them to tell the truth later. 💬 "If you are thinking about it later, you can always come talk to me about it. You can always have a redo."
- Stay neutral and calm. Sometimes a child is testing the relationship and may want to see what happens. You have the opportunity to demonstrate your care and prove to them that you can remain regulated.
- Practice and demonstrate true forgiveness and trust moving forward. This can be hard, but after a mistake or lie has been made, it's important to allow for clean slates and the opportunity to improve. If you are always questioning a child because of their history of lying, then they

may feel like there is no point in trying to improve because you will never trust them again.

- Offer praise. When a child tells a hard truth or owns a mistake they made, you can offer praise and support during these moments. Acknowledge how hard it is to tell the truth and how uncomfortable they must have felt. Reinforcing the positive choice they made can help encourage more positive choices in the future.
- Reiterate to youth that honesty from the beginning is the best way. Lies can snowball, and often the lie to cover the mistake can cause additional harm in the child's life (with school or legal ramifications).

Fear of Being Alone/Clinginess

Kids may have intense fears of being alone and want to be alongside you at all times. Even if they know you are home, they may want to be able to see and be held by you to feel safe. This is usually seen at the beginning of a placement, but it can last a long period of time and impact daily household tasks, self-care, and transitions. It may seem like controlling behavior, but I would caution you against taking this point of view. While they may be acting this way to ensure you will always be by their side, try to remind yourself of why this is happening. What looks like control is often a learned survival skill.

What you can do to help:

- Address it in the moment the best you can with gentle assurance: "I won't leave tonight while you are asleep." "I will be waiting right outside the door for you." "You are safe here." "There will always be an adult here to take care of you." You can also narrate what you are seeing 💬 "I see you don't want me to leave because you are hanging onto my leg. I know it's hard to say goodbye." Don't diminish their fears or enter into power battles.

- For transitions, use a transitional object, perhaps something of yours for them to have until you pick them up, a stuffed animal, or a small Polaroid of the two of you together. You can also draw a smiley on their hand and your hand as a reminder. As kids get older, you can give them a watch to wear and be clear on when you will be returning. 💬 "I will be here to pick you up at two p.m."
- You can ask about what they need to feel safe and come up with some ideas together. 💬 "What would help you feel better when you are in your room at night to sleep?" "What do you need at the visit?"
- At home, having children right by your side at all times can make daily household tasks more challenging. Try to find a way for them to join you in these tasks; for example, teach them to wash dishes with you or give them an activity they can do in the kitchen to stay close. For babies and little ones, try using a wearable carrier.
- You can also find ways for kids to more easily join you in different spaces in your home. Clear off space for them to be at a coffee table or at the counter in the bathroom so they can play while you get your personal things done.
- Some foster parents find visual timers to be helpful so they know when you will be available to play with them. Help them find an engaging activity while they wait for you; otherwise they may just stare at the timer and feel anxious until time is up.
- Foreshadowing can also be helpful so kids can be prepared to be away from you. 💬 "Tonight I have to work late, so Chris will be here. I won't be home until after you are in bed. Do you want me to come in

and say good night when I get home? I can leave a teddy bear in the bed with you so you know I was there."

- Over time, you can work on stepping away for a few minutes at a time. For older kids, find activities where you stay and watch while they participate (like an outdoor sport), rather than a drop-off activity.
- As they feel more comfortable without you being close at all times, look for extracurriculars with favorite teachers, school aides, or friends who provide comfort. This can be a good next step for many kids. Understand that you may need to scale back if things change in the case or with visits.
- If these separations are causing significant stress, talk with a mental health professional. Ask for parenting coaching sessions so that you can get specific advice on how to support these fears and interactions.

Taking Things/Stealing/Hiding Items

Kids of all ages may take things that don't belong to them or hide items. This can be a response to not having had their needs met on a regular basis. Youth who have had to take care of themselves or others may have had to rely on stealing to survive. Or some kids may take or hide things because they are scared that they will be taken away. Toys and possessions are important to kids, and if they have a history of housing instability, moving frequently, or having their own items stolen or sold, they may feel anxious about their things disappearing. It can be impulsive, and they may have little to no control over this. This can be a complex concern, with more significant consequences if the youth steals from stores or from others at school.

What you can do to help:

- First, put away or lock any items that are of value or sentimental to you or kids in the home. That way, you don't have to overcome your own emotional reaction if a child takes something special to you.
- For kids who are hiding things, meet them where they are by offering special places for them to keep their things safe. This could be a locking box, a drawer in their bedroom, or a special backpack in their closet for their important things. This can prevent kids from hiding things in random places only for them to be forgotten and ultimately lost.
- Lead with open communication and willingness to meet needs. 💬 "My job is to provide for you. If there's ever anything you need, please let me know." Show them you are reliable and will meet their needs (such as by keeping the home stocked with food and supplies they always have access to and always having clean clothing for them to wear).
- Try to determine the circumstances in which they feel the need to take things. Track these behaviors to see if they're related to time or day, school, peers, visits, etc. Notice if there are any patterns or triggers, and try to remedy or avoid those situations when possible. This may mean that certain places will need to be avoided during this season of learning and support.
- Get curious with them about what they need or desire, and how they are feeling when they are taking things, and collaborate on what could help them make different choices in these moments.
- Increase supervision so you can guide and redirect them when you notice they have the impulse to take something.

    - » For younger kids, you can keep items in your bag that you can use to redirect them to hold instead (make these "special" items like coins, rocks, plastic gems, and other tiny treasures).
    - » For older youth, this may include supervising them closely when in stores. Notice what they are looking at and offer to purchase it, make a plan to purchase it at a later time, or help find a suitable alternative that's within budget.
- Reflect with them about how it feels to take things and how you are there to help them find a solution. 💬 "You're saying it feels good to take those things. I appreciate you sharing that. This may be because you are feeling worried or stressed, and taking things helps you feel better." "I can help you find other ways to feel happy. Let's think about some other things you like doing." "If you want to come to me next time you want to take something, I can help you work through it. I won't get mad; I want to help."
- Punitive consequences may lead to kids being even more secretive about what they are doing. These types of consequences may also increase anxiety and fear, which can lead to more incidents where they are taking things that don't belong to them. Instead, related consequences, such as not being allowed in a store by themselves for a period of time, may be more effective. Collaborating on a plan and connecting with them to resolve the underlying need can be more helpful for youth in the long run.
- If a child expresses interest in something, validate their desires and collaborate on a way for them to work toward getting it, or something similar. Perhaps they can do extra chores to earn money, get a part-time job, request the item from a foster closet, or find a suitable alternative (like shopping secondhand).

- Give the youth an out. 💬 "If you ever have something that belongs to someone else, you can always bring it to me, and I can help return the item." Help them resolve the situation by going with them to return the item or deliver an apology letter. Make sure you are sincere and caring with this interaction, and not shaming or blaming.
- If things get severe and you are worried about consequences with law enforcement or at school, consider seeking help from a mental health professional.

Check out chapter 11 for information about hiding and hoarding food.

Leaving the Home/Running Away

This may look a little different depending on age. Younger kids may run off while you are together in public, try to get out of the car while you are driving, or run out of the house when they are triggered or panicked. As kids get older, they may wait to leave the home until it's nighttime.

This can happen for various reasons. Maybe the child was triggered by something. It could be because they wish to live elsewhere or with someone else (perhaps not understanding fully how foster care works). Some leave the home just for the night to see friends or a boyfriend/girlfriend, or because they don't like the house rules or responsibilities. And some don't know why they leave—it just happens, and they struggle to control it.

You may see kids leaving the home even after being with you for a long time. Some youth may be testing the relationship and wondering, *Do you care enough to come after me? Do you still want me?*

The goal is not to force them to stay but, instead, to create a safe environment where they feel comfortable, they want to stay, or they want to return.

What you can do to help:

- Improve safety:
  - » Use sensors on the doors and windows so you can be alerted if they leave at night. It's never okay to lock a child in their room, even young kids. Sensors on the doors and windows can be helpful for kids of all ages. You can set them so they alert your phone.
  - » Post a runaway hotline/text line so the youth can see it. Often these can be called if they are thinking about running away and also if they have already left home. Look up a hotline specifically for your county, because they will be able to best connect the youth to a temporary shelter.
  - » Ensure the safety around your home; for example, ensure that pools are fenced/secured, or consider installing a pool alarm.
  - » When out and about, hold hands or have kids ride in strollers or shopping carts. Look for parks that are fully enclosed with a fence. Find workarounds (like grocery delivery) to limit community activities that can become unsafe.
- Create support in the home:
  - » If the youth has a history of leaving the home, ask them why. You'd be surprised how many former foster youth share that no one ever took the time to ask them why they left. Don't assume what the worker has told you is the whole story. You may find that it is easily resolved.
  - » Consider being explicit about what time the youth needs to be in

the home. Some kids may instinctively just leave to walk around or go to a gas station, etc. This may be something they were used to doing without notifying an adult before they entered foster care. 💬 "We don't leave the home after 9 p.m. without an adult. If you need something at the store, we will get it for you the next day." It may seem obvious to you, but it may not be obvious to them.

- » Request a safety plan from the child's professional team, including a plan for if the youth leaves the home. You can also identify safe places for the youth to go if they do leave.
- » Keep a list of their friends and their contact info.
- » Prioritize contact and visits with family members (with permission).
- » Create plenty of opportunities for youth to spend time with their friends.
- » Make sure you know the youth's height, weight, and eye color, and any other physical features (tattoos, piercings, etc.). Keep recent photos of the youth (without a filter!) on your phone.
- » When creating house rules, consider collaborating with the youth to understand their goals and desires. By having them contribute to the rules, you may find they are more likely to follow them. If you find that there is a certain rule that isn't working for the youth, consider revisiting it. There may be a better-suited option for their age and developmental needs. The professional team can also help with this. Of course, some things are nonnegotiable (like rules related to safety).

- Remind them they can always call and text you to pick them up. Your priority is to make sure they are safe, not to be mad at them.

If a youth leaves your home:

- Try to contact them. Leaving and going out with friends is typical teen behavior, so unless there is a directive from the agency or in the safety plan to call the worker or police immediately, take a moment and try to locate them.
- If you *do* get in contact with them, you can use humor (or memes and emojis) to defuse the situation and let them know you aren't angry. Ask them to confirm in some way their location and when they will return. Compromise on a plan for when they will return home (assuming there aren't other risk factors at play).
- If you have made contact, remind the youth of the safety plan. Usually, there's a set amount of time they can be away before you have to contact the worker or law enforcement. Remind them you don't have a choice, and you can get in significant trouble if you don't follow the plan.
- If the youth can't be reached, notify the worker so they are in the loop with what's going on and what you are doing to locate them. Ask neighbors, friends, family, employers, and people from school to try to locate the youth.
- Refer back to the safety plan to remind yourself of what you need to do. Sometimes in a crisis, it is hard to think, so this plan can help you in the moment.
- If there's no response from the youth or anyone they know, update the worker and contact law enforcement.
- Go into the community to try to find the youth. Go to the places they frequent, and look for them. This is for safety reasons, but it also shows the youth that you care about them enough to go out and look for them.

There are some situations where law enforcement has to be contacted immediately, depending on the needs of the child, such as if there are concerns about abduction, suicide, or trafficking/commercial sexual exploitation of children (CSEC). To reiterate, make sure you are following individual protocols outlined by the worker or the youth's safety plan.

When they return:

- Each department has different policies about this. Some will automatically remove a child from your home if they have been missing for a certain number of days. You, as a foster parent, can always hold your home for them to return, if you wish, but not all workers will allow a youth to return there. It depends on the policy and the child's history. (For example, some workers may tell a youth that if they leave again, the consequence is that they don't get to return to that home.)
- If the child returns, let law enforcement and the worker know immediately. The worker may need to conduct an interview and require a medical appointment.
- Focus on connection rather than punishment, blame, or guilt. "I am glad you are home." "I'm glad you are safe." "Welcome back." "I have your room ready for you." "I am here to support you if you want to talk."
- Try to treat them like you did before they left. It is okay to have new rules or safety procedures, but it may best serve the youth to take it slow and have conversations over time, rather than bombard them with questions.

- Try to identify triggers or patterns when they leave. This can help the professional team identify proper support plans. Pay close attention to what happened earlier in the day (or the days prior), anything that may be happening at school, things related to their parent(s), etc.
- Connect with the child's professional team to see if therapy may be helpful.

Still struggling?

Children with intense trauma responses and behavioral and emotional considerations may need professional help. This can include therapy, medication, intensive in-home behavioral services or wraparound team support, intensive outpatient treatment, partial hospitalization, or inpatient treatment. In some situations, youth may need to move into a new foster home or a treatment center. It's important to get professionals involved so that the youth can receive the proper treatment and support.

While you are waiting for support:

- Request a safety plan for the home or at school.
- Make sure you have emergency contact information and know who to call if there is a mental health crisis.
- Take extra classes, such as mental health first aid, de-escalation strategies, or trauma-informed parenting.
- Request ongoing respite if you find you need a break to rest and regroup so you can be fully present for the child and their needs.

If the youth is admitted into inpatient treatment, explore ways you can stay connected with the youth. This could range from sending letters to sending care packages to visiting.

AS YOU ARE DOING YOUR VERY BEST, KEEP IN MIND THESE WORDS FROM A FELLOW FOSTER PARENT

"You are doing one of the hardest things a person can do—showing up with love in the middle of someone else's storm. And even when it doesn't feel like it, what you're doing matters. That child may not say thank you. They may push you away, test every boundary, and leave you questioning if you're making any difference at all. But you are. Your presence, your consistency, your willingness to try again tomorrow—those are the seeds of healing. You don't have to be perfect. You just have to keep showing up. Take a breath, lean on your people, and remember, even warriors need rest. You are not alone. And this world needs more people like you—even on your hardest days."

10

Saying Good Night

TL;DR: Supporting kids at night starts with a bedroom that is conducive to sleep, with lighting options and comfort. Tune in to their specific needs based on their trauma history so their needs can be met throughout the night. Through consistent and predictable actions, you can help kids feel comfortable sleeping in your home.

Nighttime in a Foster Home

Bedtime can be difficult for all parents. Kids don't want the fun to end, and resist or procrastinate at bedtime. They may struggle to fall asleep or stay asleep, experience nightmares or night terrors, or insist on getting up at the crack of dawn. But in a foster home, these situations can be more difficult to support because you must consider their history of trauma, neglect, or abuse, separation from parents and siblings, and difficulties that are intense, and persist and interfere with daily tasks.

If you've arrived at this chapter, you may be tired and running on little sleep. I deeply relate. Getting adequate sleep was one of the *hardest* parts about being a foster parent for me, especially at the beginning before Chris and I figured out some of the basics.

Sleep Basics from the Community

- **Offer as much choice and control as possible.** Their world may feel completely out of control. Try to find places where they get to have some power. This could be the books you read to them, how the lights are adjusted in the room, or the items they keep in bed with them.
- **Kids may feel vulnerable at night, so help them by creating a predictable bedtime experience.** Once you develop your bedtime routine, try to keep it the same every night.
- **Ensure children have enough physical activity during the day.** With all of the appointments, therapy, waiting rooms, car rides, visits, school, etc., I know it can be challenging to get in physical activity. This movement can help ensure they feel tired when bedtime comes around. A walk around the block after dinner can be a good way to get some final energy out.
- **Don't discount how important comfort items can be.** Some kids may have intense attachments to certain items, and these can be important components of a calm bedtime. The friendly face of a Squishmallow can help them feel safe and warm, their tattered lovey has been there for them through all of their hardest days, or their prized race car is the only belonging they have from home. Embrace these in your home, rather than diminishing their importance to the child.
- **Accept the fact that you are going to spend the time.** Helping kids go to and stay in bed may take a long portion of your evening, longer than your nonfoster friends spend with their kids. It isn't a race. Bedtime for kids in foster care takes time, even in the homes of the most experienced caregivers. The truth is many foster parents are staying with the kids until they are asleep or nearly asleep. Your physical presence

and your undivided attention may be what the child needs to feel safe enough to sleep. For older youth, many foster parents find that they often want to talk about what is on their mind and open up to you late at night. Build this time into the routine so these important moments don't get rushed.

- **Don't deliver bad news at night.** Sometimes foster parents receive upsetting news about the case or a family member. You wouldn't want to tell a child something significant before they go to bed and leave them to process this information alone. Consider looping in a therapist or worker and/or waiting until they have time to receive and process the information. There is a caveat to this, though. If the youth is older, it may harm the trust you have built with them if you hold back significant information from them. Be prepared to stay up with them to process and support if news is delivered at night.

Tools to Help

- ☐ **Weighted blanket:** This provides sensory support and comfort into the night. It can also feel like protection to children. Note: Weighted items (including weighted sleep sacks) are not appropriate for babies and young children. Be sure you review safety information and talk to their pediatrician.
- ☐ **Lycra tight-fit sheet:** These can be helpful for kids who need the sensory support but weighted blankets make them too hot.
- ☐ **"Okay to wake" clock:** This is a type of clock that you can program to change colors at certain times. It can help toddlers and young kids understand wake-up times. You may find that kids haven't learned sleep routines, so these clocks can aid in this teaching.

- ☐ **Sound machine or music player:** This can be really helpful to block out noises from another child in the room or house noises that may make a child feel scared at night. Make sure you check the decibel parameters for each age-group.
- ☐ **Variety of night-lights:** Kids of all ages may need a variety of night-light options. Some may want to sleep with the room relatively bright to begin with, but having smaller lights that can be individually turned on and off can make it easier to adjust over time as they get more comfortable.
- ☐ **Projector light (like a star projector light):** This can be helpful as it can serve as a calming tool or distraction for kids who have trouble sleeping. You can tell them to rest and watch the stars, rather than putting the pressure on to sleep.
- ☐ **Flashlight or handheld light:** Some kids may feel more comfortable having a handheld light they can turn on at night themselves if they feel scared, or they can use it to navigate the dark bedroom or home at night. I prefer lights with basic on-off switches, no sounds, and an auto-shutoff feature.
- ☐ **Waterproof mattress protector:** I highly suggest "double-wrapping" the bed to help with middle-of-the-night bed changes. This means having two layers of bedding already on the bed so that you can easily take off one layer if there is an accident. To do this, put a water-proof mattress protector, fitted sheet, and top sheet on the bed. Next, add another mattress protector, fitted sheet, and top sheet. Finish with comforters or blankets as needed. (Note: Check with pediatrician first about using this technique with infants)
- ☐ **Pull-up or overnight diaper (like Goodnites):** Some kids may need extra support for bed-wetting, so special underwear or diapers can be helpful.

- ☐ **Audio monitor:** Not every department will allow video monitoring systems in the bedroom, and for youth above a certain age, this isn't appropriate. Make sure you ask about policies and consider the needs of the youth. Usually audio monitors are allowed for younger children and enable you to hear if the child needs you at night.
- ☐ **Wireless doorbell system:** The youth keeps the button to a battery-operated doorbell in their room, while you keep the "bell" itself in yours. At night, if they are too scared to yell out or leave the room, a doorbell system can be effective.
- ☐ **Blackout curtains:** Even if youth need a night-light to sleep, black-out curtains can be really helpful in supporting a full night's sleep and preventing very early wake-ups.
- ☐ **Rocking chair:** Infants and little ones may feel most supported being rocked to sleep. Get yourself a comfortable rocker or glider because you likely will be spending a lot of time in it! Even older kids may want you to sit in the room as they fall asleep to "guard the door."
- ☐ **Earplugs:** Some babies, especially those who have been exposed to substances, may cry for long periods of time and have trouble sleeping. It can be hard for caregivers to rock for long periods of time with the persistent crying. Noise-reducing earplugs can help you remain gentle and present while supporting.
- ☐ **Bed tent:** This is a tent that fits on top of the bed that can feel like added "protection" for youth at night. Make sure you check with the worker before purchasing, as some may not allow this.
- ☐ **Door lock (on the inside) or door alarm:** These items may feel like added protection for youth who are worried about people coming in at night and harming them. Some places do not allow locks on the bedroom, but you may be able to get permission for privacy locks. If

locks are a no-go per policy, you can get door alarms that chime when the door opens. This can give youth a sense of security because they will be woken up if someone comes in at night.

- ☐ **Journal or diary:** It can be helpful for youth to write down their thoughts, worries, and things they wish to remember before they go to bed.

Practical Tips for Specific Situations

Bed Sharing and Room Sharing

Bed sharing or room sharing may be what the child is used to, and so sleeping alone in their own bed by themselves can be very challenging for many kids. I don't recommend foster parents bed sharing with the youth in your home. In many places, it's against policy, but it can also open the door to false accusations, or it may be triggering for the youth, who may have experienced sexual abuse. If this is a point of concern, here are some strategies that could help:

- Provide a stuffed animal that can be warmed to mimic the feeling of someone in bed with them.
- Offer a photo of their parent(s) to keep in bed with them or on their nightstand.
- Stay in the room or lie on the floor next to the bed until they fall asleep.
- Consider exchanging stuffies, loveys, or blankies with parent(s) so they have something to sleep with that smells like home. Set up this exchange at their parents' visits.
- When they cry out, go to them and meet their needs each time.
- Music, TV, or an audiobook can help them feel less alone as they drift off to sleep.

Missing Parents

If the child is missing their parent(s) at bedtime, you can sometimes set up "good night" calls with them. This can be a quick five-minute call or video chat to say good night. This can be hit or miss; for some kids it can be incredibly helpful, and for others, it can cause more distress. If they are consistently asking for their parent(s) at night and are inconsolable, it may be something you want to try if it's allowed.

Specific Trauma Considerations

If you can find out details about their history or past experiences, this can be instrumental in how you support them at night.

For Cases of Neglect

A child may have been left in their room for long periods of time, may have not been tended to at nighttime, or may have gone without sufficient food or clean sheets. They may also have slept in places like a car, park, or bathroom, and may be unfamiliar with typical bedtime routines. A baby or young child may have cried at night because they were soiled or hungry, and an adult never came to help them. These experiences can shape how the youth responds to certain bedtime routines or nighttime supports. Here are some things that may help:

- **Show kids you checked on them.** For kids who wake up in a panic or have anxiety about being left alone, consider ways to visually show them that you have come in and checked on them while they were asleep. You could leave a Post-it Note, make a note on a chalkboard that can be seen from their bed, or bring in a special stuffed animal.

If they wake up at night, this note or item will show them that you are home and you remember them.

- **Go to them if they cry for you.** This shows kids that they aren't alone and they can rely on you to help them, even with small things. A mantra that can support many kids: *No one in this home cries alone.*
- **Sleep with your door open** so the child can check at night to make sure you are there.
- **Change bedding promptly** if there is an accident or if they get sick. Don't leave kids in soiled sheets.
- **Say yes to food.** If a bedtime snack is often requested, build this into the routine. Meeting this need for food can help them feel safe. Keep a spill-proof container of water next to their bed each night. Some kids may need to be able to see the food at night, so consider keeping some food in the room if developmentally appropriate.
- **Be aware of your actions leading to bedtime.** For example, drinking alcohol or having a hushed disagreement with your partner may make a child worried about going to bed.
- **In cases of parentification, incorporate the parentified child into the routine.** Start by following their lead, and join in gently as you gain their trust.
- **Assure them of your care.** 💬 "I will be home all night." "I'm not leaving the house tonight." "I'm here to help you if you need me."

For Cases of Abuse

A child may have been abused in their bed or bedroom, or could have witnessed or heard abuse of a sibling or parent at nighttime. They could have also come out of their bedroom at night and witnessed disturbing scenes in their home.

- **Reinforce safety directly.** 💬 "Your bed is your own safe space. In this house, no one is allowed to be in each other's beds." "No one will come into your room without your permission." "Grown-ups don't hurt kids or other grown-ups in this home." Be sure you ask permission before sitting on their beds to read a story or talk to them.
- **Tell a happy story before bed** so they fall asleep thinking about a happy scene, rather than their past traumas. Bedtime stories, podcasts, or audiobooks can help with this.
- **Don't go into their room at night**, unless completely necessary. Knock and announce yourself when you enter.
- **Be aware of the noises you are making after kids go to sleep,** including the shows you watch on TV that may have triggering noises (gunshots, yelling, etc.). Kids may not realize you are watching a show and may think it's real.
- **Let them pick out what they wear to bed.** Some may want to wear their daytime clothing or shoes to bed.
- **For babies, move slowly and quietly** in the bedroom and use soft voices so as not to startle them.
- **Do not force a child to be tucked into bed.** They may not want our direct physical help with getting into bed. The same goes with hugging and kissing at bedtime. This may be unwanted or may trigger the child. You can ask first: 💬 "Do you want a hug good night, or should I wave at you from the door?"

- **Don't force or require kids to close their eyes** when you are getting them into bed. Instead, you could suggest they rest and watch a star projector if they have one.
- **Lean into preferences.** Try to set up the routine so that the preferred parent handles helping them with changing into their pj's and tucking them into bed.
- **Don't punish or discipline kids for not sleeping.** Instead, talk to them about what they *can* do if they can't sleep at night. For example, can they lie on the couch and watch TV? Read a book, or listen to music in their room? Get a snack? Being bored, restless, and alone with their thoughts at night can be troubling for some youth. The goal is to try to find ways for them to cope so they don't rely on more risky activities (such as sneaking out or self-harm). Discuss ongoing sleep troubles with a professional.

Nightmares

Nightmares are common among children who have experienced trauma. A child may cry out at night looking for their parent and be upset to find you coming in to help them. It can be heartbreaking to see kids suffer from terrifying nightmares. I have come up with a routine for myself when this happens, because I find that in the middle of the night, I do much better with a plan. I'm sharing what I do in case it helps you too:

- **Step one:** Go to them when they cry, or if they come to you, greet them gently, offer a hug, and tell them, 💬 "You're safe."
- **Step two:** Address their immediate fear (e.g., "There's a man coming into my room," "There's someone in the closet," "There's someone

coming to get me," "There's a monster"). I'll turn on a soft light in their room so they can see the space, or I'll check their space to show them it's safe while also showing them I take their concern seriously. I don't dismiss them by saying something like ✖"Monsters aren't real."

- **Step three:** Offer to take them to the restroom, get them water, or get them milk. This tends to reset the mood.
- **Step four:** Offer a back rub as they lie back down, and thank them for coming to get you.
- **Step five:** Stay with them until they fall back asleep (I find that leaving too soon can cause an escalation).

Still struggling?

If intense challenges persist over longer periods of time and are impacting their daily life and well-being, it's important to get professionals involved. A child's pediatrician, psychiatrist, and therapist can all offer different ways to support the youth with their sleep. Foster parents can play an important role in advocating for assessments and specialists. For example, you may need to add, remove, or change medications that might be impacting sleep, or there may be an underlying sleep disorder or disability that hasn't yet been identified. Consider keeping a sleep journal so you can support your observations with data. There are apps that can help you organize this information. Older kids can also assist with keeping a sleep journal to track when they are getting up at night.

Don't forget about your sleep. Being sleep-deprived and getting insufficient sleep over a long period of time can be incredibly damaging to your mental and physical health. Foster parents give so much of themselves during the day and have to recharge. Please ask your friends and family if they can come over for a night to be on kid duty, or ask for formal respite support from your worker. Your sleep matters too!

11

Snacks and Meal Support

TL;DR: Food insecurity or trauma related to food can create some elevated support needs. Focus on safe, preferred foods and slowly incorporate new options in a low-stress way over time. Create shame-free eating opportunities that consider their unique needs based on their past experiences.

Feeding Experiences in a Foster Home

In traditional homes, kids may exhibit picky eating or fuss about dinnertime at the table. They may require sensory supports or distractions like watching TV while they eat. This holds true in foster homes, but it can get more complex when you add food insecurity or past abuse related to food (such as a parent withholding food as a form of discipline). Also, stress, anxiety, depression, and other mental health needs and medications can impact appetite and eating habits.

You may need to unlearn some eating and feeding habits as a foster parent—I know I did. It felt uncomfortable at times feeding them the same thing over and over again, or providing fast food and sugary foods more often than I was used to as a kid. It was also hard to see a kid refuse to play with friends because they were focused on eating as much as possible at a party. I'm grateful for our pediatricians, therapists, and pediatric dietitians for helping me understand how trauma impacts eating and giving me a new outlook on feeding kids in my home.

Basics from the Community

Have a schedule.

Making and posting a snack and meal schedule can be helpful for a variety of reasons. Consistency, routine, and structure are all things that help kids feel safe, especially if they came from a home where they had to fend for themselves or were unsure if they would be fed. Give the youth choice and control by making the meal plan with them. Of course, when kids are hungry, you'll have to be flexible to meet their needs, even if it isn't dinnertime.

Keep "comfort foods" or "safe foods" on hand.

These are foods that are reliably well-liked and appetizing, even when the child is feeling anxious or stressed. For kids, it goes beyond comfort, as they can help their brain and body feel safe because the foods taste the same every time. Food preferences will vary and may change over time, but using input from the community, I put together a shopping list for you with common foods kids like.

> When going on outings, visiting other people's homes, or attending events, consider packing safe foods so that the child will always have something they will eat while they are away from home.

Comfort/Safe Foods

PANTRY

- ☐ Applesauce
- ☐ Bagel
- ☐ Banana/fruit
- ☐ Beans
- ☐ Bread/toast
- ☐ Cereal
- ☐ Dried fruit
- ☐ Flour tortilla
- ☐ Fruit cups
- ☐ Fruit snacks
- ☐ Granola bar
- ☐ Mac and cheese
- ☐ Noodles/ramen
- ☐ Oatmeal
- ☐ Peanut butter
- ☐ Pretzels
- ☐ Raisins
- ☐ Rice
- ☐ Rice cakes
- ☐ Ritz/saltines
- ☐ Squeeze pouches (Applesauce/Yogurt/Fruit)
- ☐ ______
- ☐ ______
- ☐ ______

FRIDGE/FREEZER

- ☐ Carrot sticks
- ☐ Cheese sticks
- ☐ Chicken nuggets
- ☐ Grapes/fruit
- ☐ Hot dogs
- ☐ Ice pops
- ☐ Jell-O
- ☐ PediaSure/similar shakes
- ☐ Pudding
- ☐ Scrambled eggs
- ☐ Yogurt smoothies

Dips/Condiments

- ☐ *BBQ sauce*
- ☐ *Butter*
- ☐ *Hummus*
- ☐ *Ketchup*
- ☐ *Ranch*
- ☐ ______
- ☐ ______
- ☐ ______
- ☐ ______
- ☐ ______
- ☐ ______

Lead by example.

You have more influence than you realize! You can teach so much by just demonstrating eating habits, trying a variety of foods, spitting out food you don't like, narrating out loud how you know you are full, and staying neutral about all foods.

Consider cultural needs and traditions.

Different families serve different foods in their home. It's important to honor the child's culture and traditions, and one great way to do this is with food! Talk to the child about what their parent(s) made that they loved to eat. You can ask their parent(s) for recipes or order something from a local restaurant until you learn how to make them in your home. This can be a great way to bond with the child and expand your own knowledge and cooking skills! Some families don't eat certain foods, like pork or shellfish. It's important to honor these restrictions.

Triple-check allergies.

Check with the worker, check the paperwork, check with their parent(s), and ask the child... Check all the places, especially for little kids who can't talk. Mistakes can be made, and things can get missed in the paperwork, so be sure to ask about allergies!

Avoid harsh rules and restrictions, unless medically necessary.

Placing harsh rules around food or trying to control eating habits can trigger a child or can lead to eating concerns in the future. In my home, we don't battle over food. It's my job to offer a variety of food options and help the child explore and consider new foods. But at the end of the day, the child needs to eat. I'd rather them eat dino nuggets again than nothing. Kids experience so much in foster care—they are put under a microscope, and their schedules can become very demanding with visits on top of school and activities. Sometimes trying a new vegetable with dinner will have to wait until another day.

If you currently have more strict rules around food with the kids already in your home, you may want to start to have family conversations about accommodations and supports for kids coming in. For example, if you have a rule that kids have to try everything on their plate, this may not be appropriate for a kid who's experienced abuse related to food. How will your family work through this together? Or perhaps a child comes back from a parent visit with candy, which you currently don't allow in your home. How will you handle this? Not every child will need accommodations related to food, but it's good to think about ahead of time.

If there are certain items you plan to use for recipes or meals that week, consider putting them in a special bin in the pantry or label them in some way. Some kids may be used to eating nontraditional food items (such as uncooked noodles or condiments) if they come from food insecurity, so it can be helpful to keep things labeled so they know what they can eat if they are hungry.

Tools to Help

☐ **Toddler stand or step stool in the kitchen:** Bring kids into the kitchen to help make meals. This is a great way to bond, and it offers low-pressure opportunities to try new things. This can also be helpful if you have a child who requires you to be close at all times. Set up the helper stool while you cook! The child can help with the meal prep, explore a new food, or even play or color at the counter with you. For older youth, get a teen cookbook and invite them to join in. Don't worry about messes or getting it "right." This is about having fun and showing them that the kitchen is a safe place to be.

- ☐ **Kid-friendly cooking utensils and tools:** Sometimes it isn't safe to use regular knives and kitchen tools for developmental or safety reasons. You can pick up kid-friendly items such as plastic or wooden knives and tools that can cut food but won't easily cut skin. Having kids in the kitchen can teach important life skills, but it can also be a good chance for them to explore new foods in a fun, engaging way.
- ☐ **Food-tracking apps:** There are a variety of food-tracking apps foster parents can use. This data can be helpful when professionals are assessing for certain diagnoses or needs. Some apps can connect directly with the therapist or dietitian, so if you are working with one, ask which one they use so you can get all the information to them directly.
- ☐ **Sensory supports:** Some kids may be physically uncomfortable at the table, which can add to challenges with snack and mealtimes. Try different kinds of booster or wobble seats, or use an exercise band as a footrest or foot fidget. Alternatively, kids may prefer to stand at the table or have a floor picnic. Some fidgets at the table may help keep their hands busy between bites. Consider putting lids on strong-smelling foods for kids who are sensitive. Divided plates and trays can be supportive for kids who are sensitive about their food touching or mixing.
- ☐ **Visual menu or choice board:** Creating a visual board can be a great way to communicate meal options and allow for choice and control.

I recommend using photos of the actual foods you plan to serve so that the child knows exactly what they are selecting. Visuals can also be supportive to neurodivergent children to help avoid possible miscommunication. You can use Polaroid photos or online templates such as those from Canva.

You may have heard the saying, "Fed is best," as it relates to feeding babies (meaning that it doesn't matter how a baby is fed—breast milk or formula—as long as they are fed). This applies to kids of all ages. While the goal is for youth to develop nutritional habits, that is difficult to do if their brains and bodies are signaling that they are not safe. In these moments, focus on safety, rather than the nutritional value of food. These lessons can come later, over time.

Practical Tips for Specific Situations

Medication Considerations

Medications can impact appetite and weight loss or gain. Here are some things to consider as you talk about this with the child's medical professional or psychiatrist.

If you know the child is starting or is on a medication that you suspect could be impacting their eating, consider keeping a food and beverage diary.

» Questions to ask:
  - How does this medication impact their eating behaviors or appetite?

- What should I look out for? What are red flags that the medication is impacting their eating?
- Are there certain foods they should avoid?
- Are there other medications or things we should be doing to help with appetite?
- Are there any specific blood tests we should request?

Limited Diets (Picky Eating)

Some kids in care haven't had experience with a variety of foods. The stress of foster care can also cause appetites and eating habits to change. This can make it difficult for many foster parents as they try to expand, and add nutrients and calories to their diet. In these situations, it can be helpful to:

- **Keep safe foods on the plate:** When offering new foods, be sure to include their comfort foods too.
- **Be casual:** Kids may not be as excited to try something new at the table, with all eyes on them. Instead, casually offer different foods during meal prep time, or when you are eating. "The cucumber tastes super fresh today. Want to try?" If they give it a try, great! But don't overreact. Stay casual. Some kids may feel very uncomfortable with extensive praise. It can feel like pressure, so try not to make a big deal if they try new things. If tasting is too overwhelming, offer for them to smell an apple or help with slicing a banana. Interaction and playing with food are a great way to introduce something new!
- **Incorporate play:** Allow kids to touch, squish, design their plate, make animals or faces out of food, etc. This creates a fun experience around food.

You may not want to use food for crafts as this could be hard for kids who have experienced food insecurity—it can be seen as wasteful, and they may want to eat the food used for the craft.

- **Use dips:** Dips are reliable and offer consistency for kids. They don't take away from the nutrients that foods offer, so go ahead and use all that ranch! Some reliable condiments and toppings to stock include:
  - BBQ sauce
  - Butter
  - Chocolate syrup
  - Hummus
  - Ketchup
  - Mustard
  - Ranch dressing
  - Whipped cream
- **Expand based on what they already love:** Take a food that the child eats consistently, and replace it with something only slightly different over time Here is an example for you:
  - The child loves chips—yum—so do I! Enjoy this food together.
  - Take them to the store and have them try other flavors of chips—this can give you some ideas of the flavors you can build into your meal options (such as cheese, ranch, taco, or spicy flavors).
  - Try tortilla chips or Doritos—this can then lead to chips with melted cheese, crunchy tacos, quesadillas, and beyond. Tortilla

chips are also good with salsa, which can help expand the foods they like.

- » Try pretzels in a variety of shapes—if they like those, you can expand to pretzel bread or soft pretzels. From there, you can try different toppings on the bread.
- » Try Goldfish or Cheez-Its—if they like these flavors, you can try expanding to cheese sticks, cheese cubes, or other cheese snacks.
- » You can also have them try crackers or Triscuits—these are salty and can be expanded with different toppings like cheese, peanut butter, or jelly.

Food Restricting

This is when a youth undereats or doesn't eat at all. Youth may restrict their eating without even realizing. Their hunger cues may have completely stopped working, so they can't properly sense when they need to eat. They may instinctively respond with "I'm not hungry," or forget to eat. Additionally, youth may have trouble noticing their own hunger cues due to sensory-related changes that are caused by trauma, or their brain may have adapted to keep themselves safe: *If I am not hungry, no one can hurt me. If I don't need food, no one can let me down. If I don't need anything, I don't need to rely on anyone. I can keep myself safe.* In these cases, it can be helpful to always have comfort or safe foods and drinks available. Setting a schedule for snack and mealtime or gentle reminders to eat can be helpful. Offering bite-size options or smoothies may also be supportive. When youth are undereating or not eating at all, this can lead to significant health concerns. Be sure you are monitoring closely with a professional.

Neglect and Food Insecurity

Create a shame-free eating experience.

Try to keep the comments to yourself if you notice them eating with their hands, eating very quickly, eating large portions, etc. Instead, you can talk about non-food-related topics or use conversation cards to help get to know each other. You can also play games (like Uno) or listen to an audiobook together. During these meals, consider eating at a slower pace, serving yourself a single portion and then going back for seconds, using utensils, spitting out food you don't like, etc.

"We will always have food for you when you are hungry. I'll show you where it is. You are always welcome to look through the food we have in the pantry or fridge. You may help yourself, or I can cook something for you."

"Even if we eat all of this chicken, there's still food in the fridge if you are hungry later."

"This doesn't taste good to me, so I'm going to spit it out."

Be mindful of your shopping and financial conversations.

Life gets busy and finances can also get tight. For kids who have experienced food insecurity or neglect, sometimes an offhand comment or an empty fridge can be troubling for kids. Even though *you* know that you will get to the store and that you can still afford food, the child may not understand this because that isn't their experience. Try your best to keep food in the pantry and fridge. Consider using meal delivery services to help when things are busy or asking a friend to help with the shopping. If money is tight, try to keep those conversations away from the kid's ears. Talking about the increased price of food may make a child feel worried about food access in the future and could cause them to stock up and hide food.

"Yes" Basket

One of the most controversial topics I've discussed online has been the "Yes" or "Anytime" basket of food. This is a basket of food on the counter, in the pantry, or in the fridge that is food the child can eat at *any* time—you always say yes when they ask to eat from it. This can be helpful when a child has experienced food insecurity. When kids have experienced that adults are unreliable, just *saying* that there will always be food may not be enough. You can help them by *showing* them they have access to food and water at any time. As they slowly learn to trust you to meet their needs, and you show up consistently and reliably over and over again, trust and attachment can form, and kids can start to feel safe again.

This may feel uncomfortable for some! You might be thinking, *Well, what if the kid eats it all and ruins their dinner?* This might happen at the beginning, especially if kids are used to not having enough food, so they eat as much as they can while there is food available. My experience is that after a few days or weeks of seeing that there will always be food, this behavior diminishes. It helps kids feel safe because they know there's always food.

Some kids may become fixated on it or want to store the food in their room. For some, especially younger children, supervision is required for any eating. With any accommodation or support, nuance matters and adjustments may be needed. That's okay!

If you find that the child is missing out on activities or struggling to step away from eating, you can move the bin. For example, instead of having it on the counter, maybe you move it to a drawer in the fridge. You can also consider modifying the timing of your meals—maybe they need an earlier dinner—or add a bedtime snack to the routine! You can also change the snacks you provide to be more filling, like full-fat yogurt, bananas, cheese, apple and peanut butter, etc. Or perhaps you need to serve more food for meals that the child recognizes and is more comfortable eating, so they are less reliant on snacks to fill them up.

Hoarding and Hiding

Kids who haven't had reliable food sources may hoard or hide food, typically in their bedroom, but they might put it in their pockets, backpack, desk at school, etc. This behavior may last a while and even a lifetime, so it may make sense to focus on support rather than attempting to "fix" it. Here are some ways to support them through this:

- **Be consistent and reliable when it comes to food.** Keep a calendar of the days you go to the grocery store and ensure you always have food in the fridge and pantry. Kids may check the fridge and pantry just to make sure they're filled, even when they aren't hungry.
- **Set a schedule for meals, and stick to it.** Serve full meals and snacks each day, and keep to a schedule or routine to enhance the feeling of safety and trust. Foreshadow and prepare the child if the food routine is changing (for example, you're going out to dinner instead of eating at home).
- **Include kids in making the grocery list, and be sure you purchase what they request.** This helps build trust and also gets kids involved in managing the food in the home.

- **Consider keeping a mini fridge, cooler, or snack kit in their bedroom.** This allows a child to safely keep food in their room instead of stashing it under their bed, for example. Add a covered trash can to their room or collaborate on a cleaning plan to keep bugs away.
- **If you find hidden food, don't shame or punish the child.** You don't even necessarily need to call it out to them. Instead, this can be a clue to you that you need to support their needs in a different way.
- **Make sure safe foods are available at all times.** Keep a bag of safe food in their backpack or coat pocket, and/or keep a drawer in the fridge or a Yes Basket on the counter that is accessible at all times.
- **Don't restrict or control food.** Putting locks on cabinets and putting limits on eating before mealtimes can trigger a child. If the child is bingeing, it may make sense to get a professional involved. If they are preoccupied with food, try keeping their hands busy with crafts or Play-Doh, or find activities outside or away from the kitchen.
- **Be patient.** I recognize this is easier said than done. Over time, many kids will start to relax and be less worried about food. Your consistent care and support are so important to instilling trust that there will always be enough to eat. They may never fully stop worrying about food during their time in your home.
- **Seek out professional support.** Disordered eating and concerns around food can be hard for caregivers to support alone, and often professionals are needed to help a child overcome them.

Weight Gain Ideas

A child may come to you severely underweight. Be sure you are checking with their pediatrician about how to best support them. A pediatric dietitian can also help support. There are some easy ways you can incorporate more calories into their diet if necessary:

- Add butter to food they are already eating (examples: under the sauce on homemade pizza, in oatmeal or scrambled eggs, on crackers, in pasta sauces, melted on chicken nuggets).
- Use full-fat milk, cheese, yogurt, cream cheese, sour cream, etc.
- Add peanut butter or avocado to snacks and meals.
- Add heavy cream to mac and cheese or pasta dishes.
- Supplement with weight gain shakes like PediaSure or smoothies with full-fat milk, peanut butter, or ice cream.
- Add a calorie-dense bedtime snack.

Concerns About Being Overweight

If the child's pediatrician is concerned about the child being overweight, work with the medical team and therapist to come up with a way to support the child. Traditional dieting for youth is often not recommended as it can impact self-esteem and body image (of course, follow all medical advice from the child's pediatrician). Instead of taking away food or restricting access, you can focus on serving well-balanced meals. Controlling or restricting food may lead to sneaking food. You can also seek out opportunities for physical activities that they love. Create new family traditions where the entire family takes a walk after dinner, enjoys bike rides on the weekend, or plays soccer at the park.

Inform the school.

If it makes sense for the child and the case, you can connect with the school about allowing access to food all day long, not restricting lunch periods as a punishment, offering private areas to eat, allowing nutrition shakes in their water bottles during class, or involving the nurse and counselor as needed.

Help them understand their body.

Sometimes when kids have been without food for a long period of time, they may become mixed up or desensitized, and they may not understand what their body is telling them in terms of hunger or fullness. You can help them by teaching about listening to your body and narrating about your own. A therapist, dietitian, or occupational therapist can also help with this.

"I can tell I am feeling full because my stomach feels tight. I'm done with dinner now."

"My tummy is making noise; it's hungry."

"I'm feeling tired, and my head is hurting; I'm going to eat something to give me some energy."

Abuse Related to Food

Food as Reward or Punishment

Generally speaking, it can get tricky if you are holding sweets hostage and requiring certain behaviors in order for a child to earn a treat, including eating veggies. This can be triggering and could create an unhealthy relationship with food. Consider using this tactic sparingly. For example, a food incentive may be needed for safety reasons, or required transitions or actions (like a visit or taking a needed medication). These aren't long-term solutions, and it's best to find new ways to encourage and motivate children, but I also want to be realistic. Going out for ice cream when a child has a major accomplishment can be totally appropriate and a fun bonding experience! Food is part of celebrations, so I am not talking about family traditions or cultural considerations.

Say yes!

Try saying yes as much as possible when it comes to snacks and meals. Whenever caregivers try to control what kids eat, this can be triggering for a child who has been punished with food. You may also consider adding things to snacks to make them more balanced (e.g., fruit snacks *and* a cheese stick), rather than saying no to preferred snack options.

Be responsive to requests.

If a child is asking about food or water, try to respond immediately as frequently as possible. I know it is tempting to say, "Not right now," or "In a minute." However, it's important to show them that their needs come first, similar to when a baby cries, especially for kids who are new to your home. Even if the child is "old enough" to make their own food, spoon-feeding a ten-year-old a bite of ice cream in a silly way or pouring a glass of ice water for a teen can be healing.

Talk to the school.

If it makes sense for the child and the case, it can be helpful to align on disciplinary measures at school. For kids who have experienced abuse related to food, encourage the school to not make snack time or lunchtime part of their disciplinary strategies (for example, if the child gets in trouble, they have to eat alone, eat in silence, or eat in the principal's office). It may also be triggering if the child has to miss a pizza or donut party because of their behavior. Ask their teachers if they implement any rules such as, "Eat healthy food first," and discuss how to opt out.

Don't force eating.

While it is well-meaning and you are trying to ensure they are getting enough to eat, it can trigger a child when you say things like, "You have to eat…" or "You have to finish…" or "You have to take one bite…"

Allow for privacy when eating.

Some youth may feel very anxious about sharing a meal with you. They may be unsure if you will yell at them about their eating habits or force them to eat something that makes them feel sick. It can take time for them to feel comfortable, so in the meantime, you can allow them to eat somewhere else in the home, somewhere private, or at a different time than everyone else.

See chapter 18 for information about food and drinks at visits.

Still struggling?

It can be really hard to see a child in your care struggle with eating. You may need to work through your own relationship with food so you can show up in a neutral and supportive way during mealtimes with kids.

If you are worried about their growth, development, mood, and behaviors around eating, I encourage you to seek out special referrals and speak with a pediatric dietitian that has experience working with youth who have experienced trauma. You can also find therapists that specialize in eating disorders and body dysmorphia. It may take extra steps to find a specialist, but it can be worth it to get proper support and care. Check out chapter 14 for more information about gathering and getting support.

12
Navigating Bathroom Needs

TL;DR: Accidents, bed-wetting, and struggling with hygiene tasks can be common trauma responses. Look for any underlying unmet needs, and offer specific accommodations based on what you find, their background, and other developmental needs.

Self-Care Needs in a Foster Home

It is common for all children to need support with potty-training difficulties, bed-wetting, struggling to learn and remember hygiene routines, or refusing to bathe. These come up in a foster home, too, but for kids who have specific trauma, their concerns can be more persistent, resulting in meltdowns and intense dysregulation or fear. Kids in foster care may require different accommodations and supports than youth who haven't experienced trauma.

In this chapter, I'm going to cover issues that may come up in the bathroom. You may have landed here because you're facing refusals, power struggles, or meltdowns about "basic" self-care tasks. I'm going to share some practical things you can try to support a child as they learn and get comfortable with these self-care tasks in your home (bathing, toileting, brushing teeth, other hygiene).

Bathroom Basics from the Community

Create an all-around friendly bathroom.

When kids move in, you may not know their background and experiences. Put your "kid and teen eyes" on, walk into your bathroom, and see what needs to be updated.

- Include kid-friendly items like a step stool, slow-close toilet seat (to help limit loud noises), toddler potty seat, nonslip rugs, easy-to-use soap dispensers, water extender on the faucet (if fostering toddlers), infant bathtub, tear-free soap, bath toys, bath bombs, and soft towels and robes, etc. Note that they may also want to bring their comfort toys with them into the bath. If it's safe, I say, go for it!
- Include sensory-friendly items like a music player, dimmable light, options for different toothpaste flavors, or adjustable showerheads.

Stock supplies.

Some kids may not want to ask for things right away, so having a cabinet or basket that is self-serve may be better suited. Stocking the basics in the bathroom can be helpful so youth can help themselves in private. This includes a hairbrush and comb, shampoo, conditioner, hair ties of varying sizes and colors, durags, bonnets, period products, tweezers, shaving lotion, hair removal lotion, deodorant, body lotion, toothbrushes, toothpaste, floss, soap, lip balm, nail clippers, tissues, hair gel or spray for a variety of hair textures, face wash, washcloths, Band-Aids in a variety of colors, dry shampoo, or shower wipes. You can take it a step further with labels on the drawers or cabinets with the child's name or be direct with a sign that says, "Help yourself to anything in this cabinet!"

Help them feel seen and part of the home.

There's a lot you can do in more passive ways to show kids they are thought of and welcome. This can include having a drawer or shelf fully cleared for them for their items (if you have a small space, you can get a bathroom caddy for them to use for their toiletries). You can also write affirmations or sweet messages on the mirror for them. Pay attention to the things they seem to notice or care about, as they may not ask you directly. You can reiterate your care for their needs:

"Feel free to use what I have, but I also plan to run to the store to pick up the brands and things you prefer. Let me know if you want to come with me or if you'd rather pick things out online."

"If I forgot something, or if you run out of anything, let me know, and I will replenish it. It's important to me that you have what you need."

Make it safe.

There can be a lot of unsafe things in the bathroom, so make sure you are locking up medications, cleaning products, sharp items like razors, or anything else that could be harmful if a child uses it without supervision or if it's ingested. For younger kids, magnet locks are typically sufficient, but as kids get older, you may need to put things behind a key lock. Think about what will help them *feel* safe, too, such as a privacy lock on the door, plenty of towels or a bathrobe to cover up.

> The youth's worker will likely have more specific directives for you if there are concerns about self-harm, sexual exploitation, or other safety needs. You may need to offer hair removal lotion instead of a razor, not allow cell phones in the bathroom, etc. Connect with your worker on how to best protect them while maintaining their privacy.

Document and report as needed.

If you notice signs of possible abuse or the child discloses abuse, be sure you are following all the mandated reporting rules in your county. If the child is completely refusing certain hygiene tasks, like brushing their teeth, it can be important to let the worker know when you start to struggle. They can help brainstorm ideas, talk to the youth about it, and also be more understanding if the child gets cavities while in your care.

Tools to Help

- ☐ **Dye-free, scent-free, tear-free products:** It may be helpful to have a variety of products that could be used by kids with sensitivities. Make sure you read the reviews, because not all tear-free products are created equally! Keep towels within reach of the shower in case kids get soap in their eyes.

- ☐ **Bath toys:** Toys can help ease the transition if the child is scared of the tub or resists bathing. For older youth, you can offer bath bombs for a relaxing retreat.

> Some bath products may irritate skin, so you may want to avoid using them for younger children, and for older youth, remind them to rinse with clear water after they are done.

- ☐ **Music player:** Who doesn't love listening to music in the shower?! This can be so relaxing and even therapeutic. Consider adding a speaker to your bathroom and giving youth the option to pick what they listen to. It can make hygiene tasks more enjoyable for kids.
- ☐ **Hygiene books and pamphlets:** These can be a great way for youth to more privately learn about their body and what it needs. You can also include resources about reproductive health or periods. Make sure the resources take into consideration the youth's gender identity and sexual orientation. These materials don't replace the work you do directly to educate the youth, but the reality is that it can take time for foster parents to establish a trusting relationship with them before they feel comfortable sharing. You can keep pamphlets in a bathroom drawer or in a basket with period products.
- ☐ **Purposeful toys:** Dolls with diapers, a bath, and a potty can be helpful in explaining diaper changes, potty training, and bathing to little ones. They may also show you through their play their fears or worries as it relates to these activities. A toy dentist kit can help you show and explain how to brush teeth or what to expect at the dentist.

Practical Tips for Specific Situations

History of Neglect

- **Show and tell** how to do things in the bathroom. They may never have been taught.
- **Take things slow and be patient.** These may be new tasks, and you don't want to overwhelm them with a ton of new information and requests, especially at the beginning.
- **Consider that these may be new or uncommon sensory situations** for them, so you may need to foreshadow and support them step-by-step.
- **Seek professional support for intensive detangling, dematting, or lice treatment.** It can take a long time, and you may not have the product and supplies in your home to properly care for hair in these situations. It's okay to ask for help!
- **Remind them that it's okay to use water,** like when flushing the toilet, including at night, brushing teeth, or bathing/showering. Some may be worried about using too much water or soap, so you might need to put them at ease with direct language.
- **Seek medical attention** for rashes, marks, or pain while bathing or using the toilet. Addressing them quickly can show that you care about their needs and that they can rely on you to take care of them.

History of Abuse

- **Offer workout-type clothing or bathing suits to wear in the bath or shower.** For kids with intense fears of bathing, you may need to use shower wipes or dry shampoo, or you could be casual and set up an outdoor pool or sprinkler for them to play in.

- **Offer to guard the door** while they use the restroom or shower. You can also show them how to use the lock on the bathroom door.
- **Prioritize independence** in the bathroom by teaching kids how to shower themselves so that you don't need to be physically present (assuming it is developmentally appropriate for them to be left alone to shower).
- **Don't assume that it's best to have young siblings bathe together in the same bath.** There may be past experiences between siblings as it relates to abuse that may make it a better experience for both if they are separated during bath time.
- **I'm sure it goes without saying, but don't take bathtub photos,** even if you think it's adorable or the child asks for a picture. Never take pictures of children when they do not have clothing on or when they are in a vulnerable position.
- **Be aware of your tone and body language if the child refuses to do something.** Perhaps in the past they were verbally abused when they said they didn't want to bathe or brush their teeth. You want to show that saying no in your home is safe.
- **Be mindful of overly complimenting or putting an intense focus on looks,** how they do their makeup, what they choose to wear, or how they style their hair. Youth may anticipate abuse after receiving compliments about how they look.

Potty Training

Foster parents who take care of toddlers and young children may be in charge of potty training. You may have heard about the "naked weekend" or "bare bottom" strategy (have the child spend the weekend wearing nothing from the waist down so they can learn quickly about their body and toileting). You may also have heard the advice to demonstrate using the bathroom. These are problematic strategies for foster families, as foster parents need to respect body privacy and trauma histories with children. Instead:

- Focus on connection and trust before starting potty training.
- Use dolls with toy potties to show what it's like, and invite the child to try themselves.
- Create a schedule for when the child will try to use the potty to build consistency.
- When you notice the child is wiggly, direct them to try to go on the toilet.
- Celebrate successes and avoid blame or punishments when accidents occur.
- Narrate or allow for choice and control when changing or undressing.
- Create a sensory-friendly environment (e.g., no surprises, no loud noises, soft lighting).
- Use padded, potty-training underwear so that kids can notice when they are wet.
- Align with their parent(s), visit monitor, and daycare provider on the plans for potty training so it's a consistent experience.
- Understand that potty training may take weeks or months, and you may see regressions if things change with their parent(s) or there are major transitions.

Daytime Accidents

There are so many reasons you may see a child struggle with daytime accidents. Being removed from their parent(s), living with a stranger in a home they don't know, intense emotions around parent and worker visits, and past neglect or abuse can all make it hard for kids to control their bladder or be able to access the bathroom during the day. This can be frustrating or embarrassing for youth, which makes this a sensitive area to support. To help them, you can:

- **Keep notes on when accidents happen to see if you can find any patterns or unmet needs,** such as day, time, what happened before or what was planned for later, etc.
- **You may need to remind kids where the restroom is in your home.** Sometimes in the moment, when it's urgent, they may forget where to go.
- **Observe and look for their body cues so you can prompt them.** For example, if they are wiggly, running around, or become irritated/elevated, these may be signs that they need to go to the bathroom.
- **Consider setting up a bathroom schedule so that they will always have consistent reminders from you.** This can help generally reduce accidents if they are regularly going to the bathroom. You can ask their daycare provider or teacher when they take restroom breaks and mimic this schedule at home too. You can also remind them to use the bathroom every time you go to the bathroom!
- **It's good to praise, but don't go overboard.** Sometimes praise can feel uncomfortable or add pressure to kids. A quick 💬 "Great job taking care of your body!" after they use the bathroom could be what they need to feel good about themselves and their accomplishments without adding extra pressure.
- **In new places, check out the bathrooms together.** This can be

especially helpful for children who struggle to use the bathroom independently due to fears or sensory challenges. Take the child to look around, check for an auto-flush, look for gender-neutral or family bathrooms, etc. This familiarity can make it easier for them to use it when they actually need to, especially if you are dropping them off somewhere (like at summer camp or a visit facility).

- **You may need to return to diapers or pull-ups.** That's okay! Don't threaten them with this (✖ "If you have another accident, you'll have to wear a diaper!"). They also sell super-absorbent underwear that looks like normal underwear, which can be helpful when kids have a small accident as they head to the bathroom. For older youth, traditional period products like panty liners or THINX underwear can be supportive for smaller accidents during the day.
- **Don't forget to pack a change of clothes**. Wherever the child goes, make sure you pack a complete change of clothing. Keep it in the car or their backpack. It can feel humiliating for kids to wear clothing that they get from the lost and found after an accident, as it will likely not fit or match. Don't forget to replenish or update the stock as the seasons change and the child grows.

Bed-wetting

This can be developmentally appropriate as they grow. Staying dry at night can take much longer than learning daytime toileting skills. Bed-wetting can also be related to their past trauma. This is a relatively common occurrence in foster homes. Here are some tips from the community:

- **Don't shame, blame, or punish.** Focus on connection and empathy.

- **Rule out any medical conditions.** Bed-wetting may also be a side effect of the medications they are taking, so ask about this!
- **Make sure they have everything they need** to go to the bathroom at night, like night-lights or a flashlight.
- **Offer extra-absorbent underwear products** (like Goodnites)
- **Double-wrap the bed with two sets of sheets and mattress protectors.** Invest in multiple bedding sets so there is less stress about a quick turnaround in laundry. Consider getting a higher-quality mattress protector that doesn't crinkle when you sit down on to create a shame-free experience.
- **You could offer to set an alarm in the middle of the night** to wake them up to use the bathroom, if the youth is interested in trying this.
- **Explain the process of cleaning up, and create systems** that are easy for the youth to do themselves (if they want to handle the cleanup independently). This includes having their own laundry bins, storing extra bedding in the bedroom, teaching them how to do laundry, etc.
- **Help them come up with a game plan** for when they are invited to overnights or want to go to camp.
- ✖ **Bribes or rewards can add to the pressure** of it all, so those types of interventions are likely not going to be effective for youth.
- ✖ **Be careful about controlling fluid intake for some kids.** Limits on food and drinks could be triggering for a child, and some need a water or bottle near their bed to feel secure.

Some kids may not wet the bed but instead go to the bathroom on the rug or in the closet in their bedroom. If that's happening, consider possible medical needs. There may be a medical condition, or perhaps they are on medication that is causing them to get confused at night or sleepwalk. Consider removing rugs in the room for easier cleanup while they are working through this. You could also offer a small toddler potty in the room if there is a strong resistance to leaving the room at night. This would at least allow for easier cleanup during this phase.

Concerns About Public Restrooms

Some children may resist the public restroom because it may be a part of their trauma history or due to sensory reasons. The experience may be overwhelming to their sensitive nervous system: intense smells, surprising and loud auto-flushes, bright lights, or loud hand dryers can just be too much for kids.

This situation can cause concern as you go into community with the child. It can cause them to run quickly out of the bathroom or refuse to use the bathroom, resulting in accidents, or become dysregulated due to needing to go to the bathroom.

- **Plan ahead.** Many places offer family restrooms, which often offer a more private, quiet experience. Many large establishments will share maps of their facilities, including restroom information, on their websites, or you can call and ask.
- **Use supports.** Offer sensory supports like nose plugs, air fresheners, headphones, Post-it notes to cover the sensor, your own paper towels so they don't have to use the hand dryers, or antibacterial wipes so they can get out quickly.
- **Offer to guard the door** or stand right outside the stall when in public so they can see your body, hand, or feet at all times.
- **Ask for accommodations** at school, such as access to a private gender-neutral restroom, or the restroom in the office or nurse's office.
- **Avoid places altogether**, if necessary, and seek out professional support.

Resisting Hygiene Tasks

Some youth may resist bathing, using deodorant, brushing their teeth, wiping, etc. This can feel frustrating as a foster parent because you may think, *The child has all of the skills and knows how to do these things—why won't they just do it?* I know foster parents are also under a microscope and can be criticized or get in trouble if the children are not bathing or caring for their teeth. It can feel like pressure added to an already tense situation in the home. So let's talk about it.

- **Uncover the underlying reasoning or need:** Get curious about what could be going on.
  - » Is this related to their trauma? Perhaps they are trying to control their hygiene and their body, or there's trauma linked to these tasks or the way it makes their body feel.
  - » Is it related to unmet sensory needs? Perhaps what you are asking them to do is very uncomfortable, and they cannot tolerate it but don't know how to talk to you about it.
  - » Are they missing some important skill or struggling with executive functioning? They may need some education or support, like reminders, visual checklists, etc.
  - » Are they struggling with their mental health? Sometimes taking care of their body is hard to do and exhausting when youth are sad or depressed.
  - » Has something happened recently that could be causing this to be a struggle? Perhaps a change in visits, something their parent(s) said to them at a visit, a recent breakup, or being bullied at school?
  - » Observe, talk to the youth, listen, and see if your curiosity can lead you to the underlying issue or need.
- **Take them shopping:** Bring the youth to the store with you and allow

them to pick out the items they think they would use. They may be worried about spending money, so you can reiterate to them that you are reimbursed for these costs. A toothbrush with their favorite character, a shampoo with a favorite scent, or a new kind of deodorant may be all the encouragement they need to use them more regularly. If needed, you can set a budget limit. Some youth may prefer to shop online, so you can offer this option too.

> If there are higher-priced items that the youth wants, such as designer makeup or cologne, you can offer some age-appropriate chores to earn money, add them to their birthday wish list, or submit a request to a local foster closet. These may not seem like necessities, but they can *feel* like necessities to the youth who may be trying to blend in with friends, or they can help them feel confident. Try not to quickly dismiss these requests, and instead, make a plan so they know you care about this too.

> Some youth may not feel comfortable asking for something or telling you when they have run out of something. You can find other more passive ways to communicate, like a journal or a digital shared shopping list.

- **Make things easy:** Stocking hygiene products in a variety of places may help youth remember to use them or encourage their use since they're more convenient. This can include their bedroom, next to the couch, in their backpack, where they eat breakfast, in the car, etc. You can also simplify processes by using 2-in-1 shampoo and conditioner, deodorizing lotions, etc.

- **Be an example:** You can demonstrate and narrate what you are doing to more indirectly teach kids, such as announcing when you need to use the bathroom, making offhand comments like, 💬 "Oh I need to put deodorant on before we go!" or "I just worked out, so I'm going to shower before I make dinner." If it makes sense for the child, you can use humor with something like, 💬 "Someone stinks! Is it me? Is it you? Let's all put deodorant on!" (Tone matters with something like this, but it can help prevent shame in the moment.)

Still struggling?

Kids may need professional intervention if they have mental health needs or have a developmental disability that requires more help with learning hygiene tasks. It's okay for you to ask for help! Some youth are more likely to take advice from adults who are not their caregivers.

13

Long-Term Fostering

TL;DR: Holidays and scheduling changes can be extra difficult for kids who have experienced trauma and are separated from their family. Navigate the child's and your family traditions with care, and be sensitive to the child's feelings and preferences during this time. Normalcy can help youth get through long time periods of waiting.

Growing Up in Foster Care

As time passes and seasons change, parents see their children grow, learn, and face new challenges. They may see increased behavioral support needs during the holidays or school breaks, when schedules and routines are all different. This is also true in foster homes. Additionally, foster parents support children as they spend the holidays away from their parent(s) and family or move homes and schools, which can cause kids to fall significantly behind in their academics. Foster parents must try to find time for normalcy with all of the visits and appointments, and they have to sit in the long stretches of waiting together with their children as the time passes slowly and kids worry about what their future holds: *Will I go home? Who will adopt me? Is my sister okay in the other home?*

Long-term foster care has its unique challenges. Kids may be with you for months or years. A lot changes during those times, both with the kids, and also with the case and their parent(s). In this chapter, you'll find seasonal-specific considerations, as well as general advice for the long waiting periods. It's a marathon. Thanks for sticking with it. Your commitment to this child will be life-changing (for both of you)!

The Basics of Long-Term Foster Care from the Community

Schedule Changes

Whenever school is out or the schedule changes, you may notice that kids in your home struggle a bit more. This could present as elevated behaviors, more intense emotions, or more resistance to daily activities. Schedule changes can also trigger a trauma response for some. Here's what you can do to help:

- Foreshadow upcoming changes directly or with a visual calendar
- Keep the meal and sleep routines as consistent as possible
- Reiterate your care for them and that you are able to meet their needs. 💬 "I know you typically get food at school, but during spring break, we will have all the food here. Do you have any requests?"
- Try to keep foster care–related appointments and visits the same so that they see the same people they are used to seeing. If they see their

siblings at school and the kids are off on a break, consider scheduling sibling visits.

Consider the child's family traditions, culture, and religion.

Different holidays or periods of time may be meaningful to the child based on their culture, family traditions, or religion. Each holiday could have specific traditions or nuances the child is used to. This is a great time to expand the knowledge that everyone in the home has of the different traditions that are important to different families. Focus on adding to, rather than subtracting from, the kids' lives.

For example, during the holiday season, perhaps the child in your home is used to celebrating Hanukkah, while your family is used to the Santa tradition. This could be a great opportunity to incorporate new music, meals, and experiences, so that everyone in the home learns something new. If there are certain things that you are not able or willing to do, make sure you plan ahead. The child's parent(s), relatives, or community members can step in to meet this need for the child.

> Align with the parent(s) on all of the make-believe characters, like Santa, the Tooth Fairy, or the Easter Bunny. Each family typically has its own unique traditions.

Hosting Tips

If you plan on hosting a large gathering, here are some things to keep in mind:

- It's good to go over the details and include the youth in the planning. They may have experienced neglect or even abuse when their parent(s) had many people over. Allowing them choice and control, and being sensitive to these experiences can help make the event a success.
- You should talk to your friends and family before attending if there are any conversation boundaries related to the child and their case. You can also let them know about any photo guidelines or what can be shared on social media.

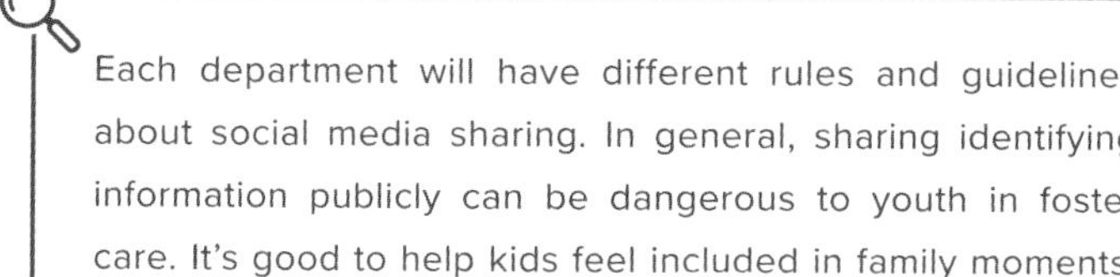

Each department will have different rules and guidelines about social media sharing. In general, sharing identifying information publicly can be dangerous to youth in foster care. It's good to help kids feel included in family moments, though! For example, it wouldn't be appropriate to ask them to step out of a photo so you can share it on social media.

- Be sure you move out of sight any posted paperwork related to foster care or the case that could be private or sensitive.
- Don't force the youth to interact or engage in specific ways. This includes coming out of their bedroom, hugs, high fives or handshakes, opening presents in front of people, participation in group games, eating Grandma's casserole, etc. Kids should be in control of their own bodies and how they engage with others. For children who have experienced trauma, pushing these interactions can feel unsafe.
- Keep the gathering to shared places in the home. This allows the youth to still have private space in their bedroom if they need it.
- Include activities that are more passive or quiet, such as a writing prompt activity, a puzzle, or a movie put on in another room.

- Consider limiting or eliminating surprises. These moments can be triggering for some youth.
- Stick to the predetermined end time. If you've told the child that the party will be done at 2 p.m. and that's when guests will leave, then stick to it.

"Sabotaging" Big Days

You may find that kids in care will "sabotage" events, celebrations, or fun activities. This can stem from trauma, so it's important to see it as a trauma response rather than a kid behaving badly. Often, they can't control this, and for some, they may not even realize they are doing it. This can happen when a child would rather be in control and lose something on *their* terms, rather than risk a caregiver or worker taking it from them. Maybe it feels too good to be true, so it's easier to stop it now so they don't get disappointed later.

What this may look like:

- Breaking a house rule
- Getting in trouble at school
- Saying things like, "I don't want to go anymore," or "I hate water parks. I never wanted to do it anyways."
- Saying they don't feel good and can't participate anymore
- Running away so they aren't there for the activity
- Telling a worker they want to leave the foster home

How to support them:

- Be neutral about the lead-up to the activity. For example, ✖ don't do a countdown or say things like, "It's in two days! Aren't you so excited!"

Instead, you may want to offer activities more spontaneously like, 💬 "It's a hot, sunny day today! Do you want to try something new, like go to the water park?"

- Make things optional from the beginning. 💬 "Saturday we could go to the water park, if you are up for it!"
- Be direct that they get to participate, no matter what. 💬 "I know things are difficult at school, but I know you are working hard. How you behave at school this week won't change our plans to go to the water park on Saturday."
- Allow for choice and control. 💬 "We have a free day on Saturday, want to go to the water park, the zoo, or have a movie marathon at home?"

"Traumaversaries"/Big Days

I personally don't love romanticizing trauma-related situations, so I choose to call these days "Big Days," but in the community, you may hear about a "traumaversary." Just like an anniversary, this is a yearly day that is meaningful and related to the child's trauma. Maybe it's the day they were removed from their parent(s), maybe it's a day they were sexually abused, or maybe it's a day that they watched their dad get arrested. In my experience, I have noticed kids' needs get bigger or more severe around the time of year when they entered my home. I've learned to anticipate these days. Kids may feel different as these days approach or on the day, and may not even realize it's happening.

How to support them:

- **Acknowledge the day.** Youth may be glad you brought it up. 💬 "I know Friday is the day that you entered foster care. It's been on my mind, and

I am curious if you are thinking about it, too," or "Sunday is Mother's Day. I know some kids want to act like it's a normal day and forget all about it, while others don't mind the day. How are you feeling?"

- **Plan for an easy day with low demands.** When the day arrives, you can offer a mental health day from school or clear the schedule of appointments, if possible. You can also build in more relaxing activities or things that require less from the child. I've listed ideas below.

Low-Demand/Easy Activity Ideas

During times of change or stressful periods, you can build easy activities into the schedule; these are things that are less demanding for the kids and often require less mental or physical energy. Feel free to use the ideas on the next page to help you get started.

Travel and Vacations

If you have an upcoming vacation planned out of state or to another country, stop reading and go notify your worker! Out-of-state travel usually requires approval. Of course, this is case- and location-dependent, but more often than not, you need to get worker, parent, and/or judge approval for vacations, especially if it's out of the state or country, or if the child will be missing school or visits. As you plan your travel with kids in your home, think about these considerations:

- **Get input from the child:** Some youth may not want to travel with you on the vacation. They may want to stay close to home, their family, and their friends, they may not like traveling, or they may not have an interest in the trip. It's good to connect with them so you can arrange for respite, if needed!

Low Demand/Easy Activities

CALM AND CONNECTED

- Reading together
- Watching TV or a movie
- Collaborative board games
- "Spa" activities like painting nails, playing with hair, temporary tattoos, playing with makeup
- Sleeping in or taking extra naps
- Casual eating (like in front of the TV) that doesn't require a lot of talking
- Easy meals that are primarily their comfort foods or meals that require minimal prep or cleanup
- Going to the movie theater
- Open or pretend play: cars, trains, blocks, kitchen, dolls
- Brain breaks or guided meditation for kids
- Bubbles
- Spending time with pets
- Picking flowers
- Puzzles
- Listening to an audiobook
- Going for a long drive

CREATIVE BONDING

- Coloring
- Decorating cookies
- Listening to music
- Painting or paint by numbers
- Sticker pages or sticker art
- Journaling or scrapbooking
- Knitting or string crafts

LIGHT MOVEMENT/ SENSORY ACTIVITIES

- Walking around the block
- Bubble bath
- Yoga
- Driving through a car wash
- Digging in the dirt or planting flowers
- Play-Doh, slime, or kinetic sand
- Water table
- Swings
- Calm bike ride

- **"Milestone" travel:** You may want to hold off on or ask about "milestone" vacations, such as taking the kids to Disney or the beach for the first time. This is a milestone moment that the parent(s) may wish to do with their child. You could ask them how they feel about this type of trip, but don't ask if you aren't willing to accept no for an answer. There are many amazing places to take a child, so you may want to take this into consideration.
- **Plan for visits:** Visits are court ordered, so you have to be mindful of them while away. You can often make up the visits before or after the trip, or do virtual visits while you are on the trip. There may be added worries from the parent(s) while you are gone, so consider creating a plan to check in with them or send photos while you are away.
- **Accommodations and support:** Planning ahead for accommodations can be helpful to keep the stress down for the child—and you!
    - » If it's the child's first time on a plane or traveling, you can show them videos or books of what to expect.
    - » Talk to the child's therapist or psychiatrist to see if there are special accommodations you need to request while traveling (such as preboarding) or if you need to refill prescriptions before you go.
    - » Look up the hospital, urgent care, and pharmacy closest to your destination.
    - » Make sure you have an after-hours/holiday emergency contact name and number from your worker in case something comes up.
    - » If you have a younger child who may run off when they are triggered, you may want to bring a stroller and/or dress them in brightly colored clothing for travel days. You can also dress in

bright colors or wear a bright hat so kids can easily find you in a crowd.

» When you arrive at the hotel or home, you may want to tour the space together and review rules or safety needs.

Travel Checklist

Below are some things you might need to bring, in addition to the standard items packed for trips (like clothing, toiletries, etc.).

PAPERWORK AND FOSTER CARE ITEMS

- ☐ Placement paperwork
- ☐ Insurance card
- ☐ Emergency contact
- ☐ Permission to travel
- ☐ Doctor's note and consent to treat
- ☐ Medication logs and daily paperwork
- ☐ Visitation device (phone, tablet, or laptop)

COMFORT ITEMS

- ☐ Loveys or blankies or other special comfort items
- ☐ Night-light
- ☐ Sound machine
- ☐ Weighted blanket or sensory items
- ☐ Parent reminders or sentimental items (like a photo of them)
- ☐ Safe food (multiple portions)

MEDICAL AND SAFETY ITEMS

- ☐ Prescriptions
- ☐ OTC meds
- ☐ Medical devices
- ☐ Babyproofing items

Practical Tips for Specific Holidays

Mother's Day and Father's Day

As you can imagine, this one is nuanced and complex! Kids may want to act like these days do not exist. They may hate these days. They may not want to celebrate you, their parent(s), or anyone, so tread carefully.

I do believe that foster parents should be celebrated in some way on these days, but try to leave that to your friends, family, or partner in your life, and remove the expectations from the kids in your foster home.

They are going through a lot. 💬 "Mother's Day is coming up. I know this day can be really complicated for some kids in foster care. I don't want to assume wrongly, so I want to check to see if you want to do anything special for your mom. I can take you shopping or help you make a gift, if you'd like. It's also okay if you don't want to do anything." Of course, some kids may *want* to celebrate their parent(s), or they may want to honor you, as well! It may just look and feel different with children from foster care.

I remember my first Mother's Day as a foster parent. The kids spent most of their day with their mom. At first, this was a little disappointing for me personally, as I had envisioned it in a certain way. I had to come to terms with my idea of parenthood being different and release my expectations of these types of days and moments. I was on a new path that could take any turn and provide new experiences that I hadn't even considered yet. We took advantage of the time without kids, and Chris and I went to the beach! We had a fancy brunch and then walked along the boardwalk. It was really special, and I'll always remember it. The kids enjoyed their visit, and so did their mom. I ended up eventually forming a nice relationship with their mother, and the children returned home a few months later. I look back feeling nostalgic as I write this part of the book. I hope that you get to have some special memories too.

Gift ideas for the child's parent(s) or for a foster parent:

- Craft or card from the child. Ask their teacher if they can make more than one.
- Flowers or potted plant. A perennial can be a special gift particularly for a foster parent, as they can remember the child each year when it blooms.
- Self-care items, like spa or mani-pedi gift card. For visits, you could pick up an at-home kit for them to do with their child.
- Photo items, like a mug, calendar, album, personalized frame, etc. I'm a sucker for nostalgic gifts!
- Something baked by the child
- Special video message, or video and/or photo montage
- Digital frame that can display photos of the child as a slideshow
- Nostalgic crafts like hand- and footprints
- Personalized jewelry or home item with the child's name or initial
- A family game to play together

> When gifting to parents, be aware of department and agency policies. Sometimes there is a spending limit, as expensive gifts could be seen as a bribe.

Thanksgiving

A day that's all about saying thanks may not be what the child needs right now.

- Consider the child's culture and traditions. Some kids might not be used to your family's traditional Thanksgiving foods or celebrate Thanksgiving at all. Remember, what constitutes a "home-cooked meal" can be different for every family and culture. Ask the child or their parent(s) about their Thanksgiving traditions and offer alternatives or culturally informed discussions.
- Connect with the child's teacher to see if there are specific projects planned related to the holiday, especially projects related to gratitude or family. This can be tricky, and it may be triggering or difficult for kids in care to express gratitude while everything around them is falling apart.
- Through the festivities, be sure you keep safe foods on hand or bring them to events. Fruit, cheese and crackers, and bread and butter are easy to include in a Thanksgiving meal.
- In some families, it's tradition to go around the table and have people share what they are thankful for. This specific activity may not make sense to do with kids impacted by foster care. Remember, it is hard for anyone to feel gratitude when they are going through a hard time in their life. Instead, if this is a tradition in your family, ask it as a general question for anyone in the group to answer if they wish.
- The day can be overwhelming with new people, food, smells, and experiences. Build in breaks and resets. It is okay to ask people to leave or leave an event early if your child is overwhelmed and dysregulated.
- Check in with the child's siblings if they are placed in other homes. See if they want to come to your dinner (or vice versa) so the siblings can be together for the holiday.
- Don't forget to thank your workers, therapists, and professional team!

It's a good checkpoint to express your own gratitude for the work they do to support you and the child.

The Holiday Season

This can be a difficult season—change in schedules, increased excitement may bring increased trauma responses, different triggers, and more. It isn't always "the most wonderful time of the year" for youth in foster care.

Coming together and incorporating everyone during the holidays:

- Ask the child and their parent(s) about their wishes, desires, and boundaries.
- Find space in your home to allow the child to decorate and showcase their traditions.
- Ask the family about recipes, or purchase the family's traditional holiday meals from a local restaurant.
- Make plans for a fun alternative if a child is not participating in certain activities.
- Find community members to help incorporate the child's cultural and religious traditions into their life.
- Add the child's favorite holiday songs to your family's holiday playlist.
- If parents are not visiting, ask about visits with relatives to maintain family and cultural connections.

Foster parent considerations:

- Understand that the child's experience with the holidays in the past may have been related to trauma or instability. Consider their traumatic experiences as you move through these weeks.

- Make sure you align with your friends and family about gift giving. Kids in foster care should get the same amount/value of gifts as your permanent children in the home.
- Try to get to know the child, and purchase gifts based on their interests. Youth know the difference between a generic gift vs. a gift they would actually love. I know this can be difficult for new kids in the home, but remember that it's okay to ask! They may enjoy picking out their own gifts.
- Remember that everything the child is gifted leaves with them when they transition out. If you want to purchase a large item that will remain in the home after the child leaves, like a video game system or tablet, make sure you make it a "family gift" not an individual gift for the child.
- Don't threaten or withhold gifts because of a child's behavior.
- Foreshadow or create a social story about the holidays and festivities.
- Help them with shopping for their parent(s) or siblings.
- Consider the schedule and how many people they will be visiting or having in the home. This can get overwhelming and exhausting during an already hard season.
- Prioritize rest and downtime to process or decompress.
- Consider the child's common triggers in a holiday context (for example, Santa may be scary if the child has experienced trauma at night or with strangers).
- Coordinate with the child's teacher ahead of time to ensure that holiday projects are considerate of the child's family dynamics.
- Pack safe foods to have available at parties or festivities.
- Do not require hugs or physical interactions.

- During the holidays, the kids may receive gifts from the department or agency, their CASA, parents, or other professionals working with the youth. They will likely ask you what the child wants. This is a good time to *also* ask if they will be bringing a gift for *all* of the children in the home. It can be hard for some kids to understand why only the kids in foster care are getting gifts. You may want to make a plan for how to support this moment.

If you have space for additional children in your home during the holidays, you may want to send this reminder to the worker or the placement office. Sadly, there are many removals and disruptions during the holidays. If you are available, let someone know.

Birthdays

- First, make sure when you get the placement call, you ask their birth *date* (not age). You may find that kids enter care on or around their birthday.
- You can keep general birthday supplies on hand so you are always ready, and this can help save you time and money for the various birthdays you will celebrate! This can include:
  - » A bag of balloons
  - » Streamers
  - » Birthday candles
  - » A neutral (no popular characters) "happy birthday" sign that could be repurposed for anyone
  - » Birthday hats

- Different ages mean different things for various cultures and religions. Be mindful of these milestones and connect with their families or a community member to help support and celebrate with the youth! With that, for many parents, across cultures, the first birthday is a milestone moment. You may want to consider something special for this day, such as an extra visit or sending pictures or videos.

> If something special can't be arranged, you can connect with the parent(s) about bringing a cupcake to the visit so they can be part of the baby's first cake experience.

- For older youth, start by having an open and honest conversation about their preferences, triggers, and boundaries. Create a safe space for them to share their feelings and concerns regarding the celebration. Empower them to have a voice in the planning process and make choices that feel comfortable to them. "Some teens love celebrating their birthday, while others don't want any acknowledgment of the day. How are you feeling?"

> Some may share that they wish to skip or forget about their birthday. I know this can be heartbreaking, but respecting their wishes can be very important. You can consider having a card or gifts at the ready in case they change their mind last minute. You can also ask them if you could give them a few gifts or take them to their favorite restaurant on a different day.

- It may not make sense to have the child open gifts in front of others. They may not have the social skills regarding how to respond if they don't like the gift, they may feel uncomfortable, or they may not express gratitude.

- If you are hosting a birthday party, consider including their parent(s) (if the child wants this and it's allowed).
- Consider adding their birthday to your digital calendar to repeat each year. I like doing this because if they aren't in my home anymore, it gives me a reminder to pause and send good vibes to them, and it can also be a reason to reach out after reunification to say hello and offer to send a gift (if you still have a relationship with their parent(s) after reunification).

The "In-Between" Times

Kids may stay with you for a few hours or a few years (or a lifetime, if the case moves to permanency with you). If you are providing longer-term care, you will be fostering in the "in-between" times, when their parents are working their case plan and the child's future is largely unknown. *Will they reunify with their parent(s)? Will a different relative come forward to care for them? Will the department seek permanency with you? How long will the process take, and when will you have answers?* Providing normalcy during this time is a challenge, but do the best you can so kids can be kids.

Seasons of Waiting

Waiting is hard and uncomfortable, and uncertainty can make daily life difficult. It can be challenging for the foster parent and the child. During these waiting times, you can:

- **Focus on short-term plans** like this weekend or this month. This can help keep your mind busy, and you can still look forward to something as a family. Making plans can be fun, but try to make them short-term.

- **Have more everyday family traditions.** Don't wait for birthdays or holidays to incorporate family traditions. Having more frequent family traditions can help everyone move through the days and take focus off the stress of foster care and the *what's gonna happen?* thoughts. Some examples: Ice Cream Sundae Sundays, Pizza Fridays, going to the movie theater each time there is a new family movie, a stroller walk after dinner each day, stargazing on clear nights, spending time each weekend cooking a new recipe together.
- **Acknowledge questions and needs.** When questions come up and you don't know the answer, instead of just saying, "I don't know," let the child see you add it to a list of questions for the next worker visit. This is a way to physically show kids that you care about their question and concern, and that you will work on an answer. Pull the list out when the worker or their advocate visits. They may, at some point, finally have an answer, so it's good to keep track of these questions. The act of writing it down can also feel like a release from your mental load, and the child may feel this too.
- **Set short-term goals with the youth.** Just because you are waiting on parents to reach their goals doesn't mean the youth has to stop their progress in life. Ask them what goals they have, what they want to learn how to do, what they want to work toward being able to buy, or if there is something new they want to try. Foster parents have an opportunity to help set kids up for success and to achieve their goals. It's a wonderful thing to witness!
- **Celebrate small wins.** A win is a win, and small moments of growth

and strength should be acknowledged. Each child will have different ways they like to receive praise or acknowledgments. Celebrate trying a new food, finishing a chapter book, attending therapy, or talking through a sibling conflict rather than yelling. There can be so many negative things thrown at kids in foster care—make sure you take time to acknowledge the good.

For youth who struggle with self-love or have low self-confidence, it may be hard for them to accept compliments, or praise may feel like pressure and be uncomfortable. For these situations, you can be more descriptive or declarative.

"You did it." "It was a tricky situation to navigate, but you made healthy choices." "I noticed that each week you've been getting a higher and higher grade on your times tables. Those are really difficult, and you haven't given up."

- **Take time to understand procedures.** Sometimes when foster parents understand procedures and steps, it can help everyone feel more settled. For example, ICPC (Interstate Compact on the Placement of Children—this is for when a child's case is being transferred to another state) may take a few months to over a year, but there are steps throughout the process that you can track along the way. Talk to their worker or advocate if you have questions about certain child welfare procedures. By understanding the process and steps, you can feel more at ease, and the youth may also feel more at ease knowing what is going on.

The Ups and Downs and Surprises

Foster care is full of the highest highs and the lowest lows. You may have one case that ends in a happy family reunification, and then you may have another case where the youth runs away and the worker doesn't allow them to return to your home. Case plans can change seemingly out of the blue, from reunification to the kids moving across the country to live with a relative.

- **Find joy in the day-to-day.** Because tomorrow is not promised, try shifting your mindset to the present. Appreciate and love the child as they are today. This is easier said than done sometimes, especially when you are in the thick of it.
- **Keep a "maybe" mindset.** When talking about the case or foster care–related concerns with the youth, make sure you aren't promising anything that you are not certain about. If you show that you are comfortable with "maybe," it will help them be more comfortable too. You can come up with backup plans together if that helps them feel more settled with maybes. For example, if the youth is hoping the judge approves for them to live with their aunt, you can share that the backup plan would be for them to live with you and that you can create a plan to visit with their aunt. A helpful household mantra you can use: *Change the plan, yes we can!*
- **Reiterate things that are not changing right now.** When kids are processing changes or surprises, it can be helpful to remind them of things that will stay the same, such as their teacher, their worker, or your steadfast care for them.
- **Disappointing or bad news.** There may be significant news that the child needs to be told, that you know will be disappointing or cause the child considerable concern or sadness. Ask the worker if they plan to

deliver this news themselves, or if you or the therapist will be doing that. For some children, a coordinated group effort may be important so they can feel very supported in the moment (such as the death of a parent or sibling). Alternatively, sharing smaller, more digestible bits of information over time may be easier for kids to process, understand, and accept.

Try not to give bad news before bed, as this is already a vulnerable time for kids. Even if they say they are okay, they may stay up late wondering and worrying alone. Of course, in some situations, like with older youth, it may be damaging to your relationship if they know you held back important information from them. It's a balance!

Normalcy

Providing normalcy is an important part of fostering. You don't want kids to miss out on typical childhood experiences and traditional opportunities for growth and development. In plain terms, this means extracurricular activities, time with friends and dating, summer camps, and even things like household chores and responsibilities, getting a job, or learning to drive. Here's a brainstorm of ways to incorporate normalcy into the child's life:

- **Vacations and travel:** Traveling with children in foster care is usually allowed and can be an incredible experience for kids in foster care. Of course, you do need the proper permission. If you aren't allowed to leave the county, consider adventures at a local museum, going for a new hike, or exploring new restaurants or art galleries.
- **Extracurriculars:** These are a great way to enhance normalcy while

also ensuring the kids have time to connect with peers, explore a hobby, and beyond. This could include sports, after-school programs, summer camp, school events, and clubs.

- **Being with friends and dating:** Being around peers can often be incredibly supportive to kids in foster care. Dating is also an important part of being a teenager, and you have an opportunity to be there for them, provide sex education, and guide them in making responsible decisions.
- **Cultural and faith-based activities:** This can include attending community events, having visits with extended family members, participating in milestone events, creating opportunities to hear and speak their family's language, eating cultural food, and beyond. Having a strong cultural identity is really important for kids in foster care. Additionally, youth may feel disconnected from their faith and may benefit from your efforts in connecting them with faith-based supports or helping them attend religious services.
- **Household responsibilities:** While chores are no one's favorite thing, it is a normal part of growing up! Having household tasks can help kids feel a part of the family and help them feel like they contribute something in the home. It's sometimes easiest to assign responsibilities based on the child's strengths and interests. For example, if they love the family pet, maybe it's their responsibility to keep their cage clean or take them for a walk.
- **Tech/screen time:** I know that it can feel like a whole other job monitoring and keeping track of tech and social media usage. However, playing video games with friends, using their phone, etc., are a part of growing up. You have an opportunity to teach kids about how to be responsible and safe online.
- **Self-care:** Having an appointment every single day and feeling like

there's a microscope on them at all times can be incredibly draining for youth. You can advocate for time off from appointments or finding a day or two each week to not schedule anything. Allow kids to lounge around, relax, play video games, etc.

- **Getting a job:** Help the youth create a résumé, practice interviewing, fill out applications, and support them through the ups and downs of having their first job. Consider writing a reference letter for them and helping them find other adults to use as a reference.
- **Learning new skills:** Foster parents can play an important role in teaching new skills, like learning to swim, riding a bike or scooter, throwing a baseball, learning to drive, playing a musical instrument, etc.
- **Prepping for independence:** Teach youth how to do laundry, manage money/their allowance, how to cook, how to fix things around the home, etc. You can make a huge impact by taking the time to teach and having patience with mistakes.

Talk to the child's worker or advocate about getting additional funds to pay for these activities and extracurriculars. There may also be nonprofits in your area that can help with these requests. I've also had success asking for scholarships directly from the organization (assuming the youth is okay with you disclosing they are in foster care).

It may feel impossible at times figuring out how to schedule these into an already demanding schedule. There may be intense time periods where these types of things are not prioritized, and that is okay! Please come back to this part of the book in a few weeks or months and try again. It's important, but it's okay to be realistic.

14
Gathering and Getting Support

TL;DR: If foster parents aren't supported, it can be really difficult for them to support the kids in their home. Burnout is a real concern and can have a devastating impact on the foster parent and the kids in their care. Prioritize self-care and asking for help.

When Tired Turns into Complete Exhaustion

Many parents have seasons of burnout and exhaustion. The demands on modern parents are intense, and it is common for families to struggle during times when their kids have elevated behavioral or emotional needs. Work life balance is a myth, and families don't always have strong, reliable support. This is also common in foster homes, but things can get really severe for some foster parents. Compassion fatigue (emotional exhaustion from caring for others), blocked care (suppressed feelings of care to protect yourself from emotional harm), secondary trauma, ambiguous loss (unclear loss without closure), grief, and burnout can lead to foster parents disrupting placement or quitting all together. You will likely hear throughout this process "You have to put on your own oxygen mask first before you can put one on the child." This saying came up in almost every training, and honestly, I got tired of hearing it. I didn't realize how essential it was.

This is an important chapter that I hope you take the time to sit with. Most foster parents will face difficult parts of their foster care journey where things become so overwhelming or discouraging that they need help from a support group, respite provider, friends and family, foster parent mentor, or a mental health professional. Even foster parents with the best self-care plan can experience some serious mental health needs.

Protective Factors

There are many things that foster parents can do to protect their mental health as they foster. Foster parents in the community found the following to be supportive to their well-being.

Structure and Routine

This isn't just good for the kids, it's good for you too. It can help reduce decision fatigue and clear up some of the mental load of parenting and fostering.

Set up regular babysitting.

This is hard, but I encourage you to try to set up regular babysitting so that you can get a break. Getting a babysitter can be triggering for some kids, especially those who have experienced neglect or abuse when strangers were in the home. Take this slow by having the sitter come while you are there, and then have them watch the kids for short periods of time.

- If this is still difficult for some kids, you can try having a sitter come at bedtime so that the children are already asleep when you leave the home. When Chris and I did this, we would schedule the sitter to arrive a bit before bedtime to say hello to the kids, and then sit and read on the couch while we did bedtime. That way the kids saw the sitter and knew they were there (so it would not be jarring if they woke up and the sitter was there to help), but the kids got to keep the routine they were comfortable with and were asleep before we left for a late dinner or movie.

- At times when that solution still did not work for the kids, Chris and I would take turns leaving for the evening to have dinner with a friend, while the other did the bedtime duties solo. This was still hard, but the more we did it, the more the children became comfortable with one of us being out for an evening.
- You may also have more success with sitters in the morning, when kids are "fresh" and have more tolerance for something different.
- Regardless of what technique you try, the key is to try. Not having childcare or the ability to use a babysitter is really hard. Likewise, for the kids, being able to adjust to a babysitter is a skill, so it may take several "practice" attempts before they get used to the babysitter routine.
- If you need specialized sitters, there may be disability services in your state that can provide a higher level of childcare, or you may find a drop-in childcare center that could be more supportive for kids. Sometimes the drop-in centers feel more like playtime.

Scheduling Self-Care

Try putting the times you are planning to devote to your hobbies or interests on your calendar, like getting to the gym, going on a hike, or seeing a local concert. If it's scheduled and written on the calendar, it may be more likely to happen.

Engage your friends, family, and community.

I know it can be hard to ask for help, but if you aren't continually getting support from your community, foster parenting may not be sustainable. 💬 "I'd love to get something on the calendar for us to get together. I could use a venting session! Want to grab lunch next Wednesday?" If you can't see friends in person, exchange voice notes or jump on FaceTime for that personal connection. A trusted friend can be important to help you process what you are experiencing in your home. Being involved in community groups, such as fitness communities or religious organizations, can be another place to get support and care.

Attend foster family events or support groups.

Many departments and agencies will host special events or support groups for foster families. These gatherings can be a great way to feel less alone. Everyone there is going through what you are, and I find that the families and volunteers there are always gentle and flexible about what the kids need. It's also a great place to meet other foster families and start to form these friendships and connections.

Get support from a foster parent mentor.

In some places, there are formal mentorship programs for foster parents. I have worked with a foster parent mentor a few times, and it's always been very helpful. Typically you chat with them once a month or more often to talk about what's going on, vent, or get advice.

THESE SUPPORT GROUPS CAN BE LIFE-CHANGING. ONE FOSTER PARENT SHARED

"A monthly support group for foster moms was literally the reason I was able to continue in our foster care journey during the height of our hardest season. Knowing you aren't alone, knowing people who 'get it' are there when you need it, and being able to lean on that support is invaluable. Having people invested in my life and cheering on my kids was one of the most valuable investments to come out of that group, and we survived because they held us up when we felt like we were drowning."

Affirmations

I know in my hardest of seasons, I can get down on myself. I want to offer you some positive affirmations for you to repeat to yourself on hard days. Some of my community members have shared these with me, so I'm passing them along to you:

- It's okay to take time for myself. Taking care of myself helps me take care of others.

- I am a safe place.
- I am an important part of this child's path to safety and healing.
- I can provide care and comfort, even if I am not in control.
- I have not failed when things are hard.
- I am proud of how far I have come and how much I have grown. I am still growing.
- I will find a way through. I always do. That is my strength.
- The stability I am providing is meaningful.
- I am brave, and I can weather this storm.
- Even when my voice shakes, I can be heard.
- I play an important role on this child's team.
- I can center the child, even when the system doesn't.

When Things Get Severe

It's good to take note of how you are feeling and notice some possible red flags that might signal a more significant mental health need.

When you are so "over it" mentally and physically, and the stress of it all has been pounding down for such a long time, and you start to wonder *Is this sustainable?* you might get so drained that you may find it hard to really care anymore. You're living with the effects of trauma on a day-to-day basis, which can be incredibly challenging over a long period of time. Perhaps you've experienced primary or secondary trauma. You may feel like giving up or like you just don't have anything left in you. The child may be telling you every day that they don't like you, don't want to live with you, and refuse to engage with you. Maybe you are starting to feel that way too…

In addition to these feelings, you may be experiencing signs of greater mental health concerns. For example:

- Ongoing, persistent trouble with sleep
- Feeling anxious in a way that impacts your daily life
- Forgetting important foster care tasks
- Getting behind in paperwork or foster parent responsibilities
- Feeling overwhelmed by small things that didn't use to feel as upsetting
- Feeling short-fused or quick-tempered, yelling more
- Isolating, preferring to stay home more often, not wanting to go out and about with the kids or attend a support group
- Crying more often than usual, not being able to control emotions during team meetings or parent interactions
- More frequent or new physical health problems impacting day-to-day activities
- Neglecting your own needs to the extent that it's starting to impact daily life
- Not accepting input, advice, or extra services to help; maybe you say: "I've tried it all. Nothing will help."
- Inability to find joy in the day-to-day or struggling to have fun with the kids
- Loss of hope or purpose for fostering
- Avoiding interactions with the professional team or parents
- Inability to keep up and maintain a compliant, safe home

I say this gently but with a tone of urgency: This level of burnout and exhaustion can prevent you from providing proper care to the kids in your home. Please keep reading to learn how you can get help.

Getting Help

Many foster parents and people working in helping professions have been where you are *and* they were able to turn things around, change their circumstances, and get back to a neutral state.

Consider the following ways to get help:

- **Additional support from the department:** Be honest with your worker about what you need to make foster parenting and caring for this child sustainable. This could be transportation support to and from school, visits, or other appointments. You could also ask for assistance with monitoring visits (if you are currently managing this).
- **Respite:** Getting respite care for the child can be very supportive during this difficult time. You can request ongoing respite (like one weekend a month) or request a full week so you can have several days of processing and rest. Depending on your agency or county, it can take some time to arrange this, and not every provider will be a fit for the youth. I share some respite considerations in the next section.
- **Intensive in-home services:** In some places, you can get intensive home-based services where behaviorists and therapists for the child come directly to your home. These services are there to help the child and help you get through this difficult period. Some areas also call this service "wraparound" or "therapeutic behavioral services." Asking for this level of help does not mean you are a bad foster parent. I've participated in these services a couple of times. Each time I hesitated to ask for the referral, but I was always glad once the services began. I felt less alone and isolated, and the child was getting the help they needed.
- **Therapy for you:** There are many different options for therapeutic support from a mental health professional. Some therapists offer

telehealth therapy, which may be easier to fit into your busy schedule, and it opens you up to many more providers in your state. You can find therapists that specialize in areas like grief, trauma, anxiety, or depression.

ONE FOSTER PARENT WHO'S BEEN IN THE TRENCHES SHARES THIS ADVICE

"I didn't start therapy for myself until my first was actively reunifying, but it has been *so* helpful to have a safe space to process through the spectrum of emotions in this process. It can feel so guilt inducing to grieve reunification when you know that is the goal, and the weight of saying and doing all the 'right' things is so challenging when you are prepping for goodbye. It's wonderful to have a supportive community, but it's another type of support to have a professional listening and helping you process."

A Closer Look at Respite

Understand how it works in your area: Respite care is when the child stays with an approved caregiver. It's typically overnight care for several days, but in some places, you can get respite for just a few hours.

Sometimes you can have a friend or family member provide respite care. This is usually an optimal solution because they aren't a total stranger. Ask your agency/department what is required of babysitters and respite providers. They may need to undergo a background check or complete first aid courses. Respite care with another foster family is often paid for by the county and there's no additional cost for the foster parent.

Foster parents typically request respite for a variety of reasons. Some examples are for travel purposes when the child is not approved to go (or it's not appropriate for the child to go), a medical reason, work commitments, or when the foster parent needs a break for personal reasons, to reset and focus on self-care.

Talking to the Child

Respite can be hard for kids. You are asking them to stay with a stranger, and they don't have a lot of control over the situation.

It's important when communicating with the child about respite that you make sure you don't blame the child. Yes, sometimes foster parents need a break to focus on self-care, but you don't want the child to feel like they did something wrong or to feel like they are in trouble. 💬 "Next weekend, I have to take care of a few personal things so you will be staying with another foster parent for two nights."

It's important you don't send foster kids to respite while you go on a family vacation (unless the child has indicated that they don't wish to go on the trip). It can be isolating and hurtful to be left out. Consider going on vacations before starting to foster or in between placements. Sometimes approvals from the county fall through or parents change their mind about allowing travel to happen.

Before Respite Begins

If you don't have a friend or family member who can step in to be a respite provider, your worker should be able to help you find someone. Due to limited available foster parents in many areas, it can take some time to identify a provider. Once a respite provider has been found, it can be helpful to speak with them beforehand. Consider asking:

- How long have you been fostering?
- Do you have experience with this age-group?
- Do you have the right bed, car seat, stroller, toys, etc., for this age-group, or do I need to provide any equipment?
- What is your experience with kids with this disability, medical need, or background?
- What are your views regarding discipline, or what are your discipline practices?
- Are you comfortable monitoring parent calls?
- Is it possible to arrange for you to have a phone call or video chat with the child beforehand? Could I see a photo of the room they'll be staying in so I can help them prepare?

Aligning beforehand can help set everyone up for a successful respite experience.

Packing List

Connect with the respite provider to ensure they are providing food, snacks, supplies, etc. Don't assume. You'll also need to pack:

☐ Clothing, underwear, socks, shoes, hoodies, etc.

- ☐ Pajamas (potentially more than one set if bed-wetting is a concern)
- ☐ Personal care items like a toothbrush, hairbrush, deodorant, period products, etc.
- ☐ Medication
- ☐ Medical equipment
- ☐ Paperwork including contact info for you, the worker, the emergency contact, medical documents, the safety plan, etc.
- ☐ Comfort items such as loveys, stuffed animals, blankets, weighted blankets, fidgets
- ☐ Favorite snacks or safe foods
- ☐ Baby care items such as diapers, wipes, formula, bottles, pacifiers
- ☐ School items, projects, homework
- ☐ Night-lights, sound machine, any other must-haves for sleep
- ☐ Bag for dirty clothing
- ☐ Coats, swimsuits, boots, anything needed for special activities

Don't forget to label everything. This can be especially helpful if they are visiting a home with other kids.

Invite the kids to help you pack. Having them see what you are packing may put them at ease so they know they will have their personal items. I don't recommend bringing sentimental items unless they're absolutely necessary for comfort. Having those items get lost or broken can be devastating.

Checking In

While the child is in respite care, it can be helpful to check in with the foster family and the youth to help put them at ease and make sure there isn't anything they need. You don't want kids to feel deserted and forgotten.

You can also leave a note in their bag for them to find later, letting them know that you are thinking of them. Younger kids may be confused and need the reassurance you are coming back for them.

After Respite Care

After the child returns back to your home, it's good to follow up with a few questions, especially if respite will be an ongoing resource for your family:

- What did you like best about their home? What did you like least?
- What was your favorite moment? Least favorite moment?
- Was there anything you needed that you didn't have?
- Would you like to visit them again if I ever have to travel in the future? Why or why not?
- Anything else I should know?

Providing Respite

Providing respite can be a helpful way to begin for some new foster parents. It's a way to get parenting experience and start to get to know how the system functions before committing to being a full-time foster parent. There are also some foster parents who go from traditional fostering to being just a respite provider, as it is a smaller (but still very important) commitment.

If you are planning to provide respite, here are a few quick tips from other respite providers from the community:

- Try to get as much information from the current foster parent about the child as you can: what they like and dislike, their daily routines and schedules, how to help them when they are upset, medical needs, etc. You can offer to video chat with the child to break the ice before they arrive. Some respite providers will also do a short playdate in the home before the respite stay.

- Stock games and toys that have broad appeal, such as art supplies, building blocks (like magnet blocks or LEGO sets), outdoor games/equipment, slime or kinetic sand, stuffed animals, games (like Uno, Jenga, picture charades, or puzzles).
- Allow for as much choice as possible. Respite is just one more thing that is out of the child's control, and you are another stranger in their life. It can be a lot! Choices can help kids feel more in control.
- It's good to plan activities during the child's stay, but try to keep plans flexible and offer a variety of options. Once they arrive, allow them to choose what they want to do. Provide optional activities around the home (like doing craft kits, watching movies, playing in the backyard, or baking) and options for community activities (playing at a park, visiting a zoo or library, or going on a hike).
- Be open to ordering takeout and/or offering some packaged food options, as these are reliable and taste the same each time. Eating in new environments can be difficult for children, so try to keep it simple and offer things they will easily eat.
- If allowed and the youth is okay with it, consider taking photos or videos of the kids during their stay. This can help put foster parents and parents at ease.
- Remember to maintain the standard foster parent responsibilities, like daily paperwork, documenting and reporting injuries, taking kids to school, appointments, and visits, etc.

> I want to be really transparent. Sometimes things don't happen how they should when it comes to providing respite. Sometimes kids get to you and beg to stay, and share that they are being mistreated in their current home. Sometimes the worker is trying to move the child but can't find a permanent home for them yet. These situations are less common, but they do come up. Try to get a clear picture of what the worker plans to do before you accept.

Disruptions

Sometimes the needs of the child or the case are greater than what you and your family can provide. This is often a devastating end to a placement and can leave foster parents feeling unsettled, guilty, and questioning if they should continue fostering.

Other times, the worker may choose to move the youth from your home if they feel they need a higher level of care or different dynamics in the home. Or the youth may want to move to a different home for a variety of reasons.

If you have decided to disrupt placement, there are things you can do to make this as smooth as possible and reduce the impact of trauma the best you can:

- **Consider telling the worker as soon as you know and in writing.** In many places, there is a timeline in how long the worker has to find a new home, so having this in writing can align everyone on what to expect.
- **If at all possible, try to allow for the proper amount of time for a**

suitable home to be found. While a time limit is important, so is the right amount of time to find a suitable replacement home. Try to balance this the best you can, keeping the child's safety in mind.

- **With that, you can offer to help find a home by reaching out to your community,** making the child available for meet and greets, or being open to talking to possible foster parents about the child's needs.
- **Talk with the team/therapist about how to best inform the child.** This can be a traumatic event for the child, so handling it with care is important. You can consider opening the door in a variety ways such as, 💬 "I wanted to let you know that we have to make some changes in our home. This will mean that you will have to move to a new home in the next few weeks. I want to support you through this, so I'm committed to doing everything I can to make sure your new foster parent is a great fit."
- **It's important not to blame youth.** They will likely ask why, so be prepared with what you will say. 💬 "We have to take a step back in fostering and get additional training. We have a lot of personal responsibilities that are interfering with the care that we are able to provide. We want to ensure you have a caregiver that can provide you with everything you need."
- **Empower the youth to share their desires.** If the child wants the move, work with them to articulate their needs and desires in writing, and then share that with their worker and advocate (attorney, CASA, or GAL). This can be helpful to find the best suitable home for them and a great opportunity to help empower them to speak out about their needs.

To help with the transition:

- **Try to be as flexible as possible in supporting extra visits with the new foster parent.** You can consider having the child move their items little by little, over a few visits, for them to start to get acclimated.
- **Try to organize the services as best as possible for transition.** Once the plan has been finalized, create a contact list to share so that the new foster parent has all of the info at their fingertips. Inform the professionals of the change so that they can adjust their care and conversations with the child.
- **See if the therapist thinks it's a good idea to increase sessions during transition time.** Look to the professional to direct you on what they think would best support the child. It may also be helpful to get the school counselor involved during the transition time to check in on them and show support during the day at school.
- **Give as much control and choice to the youth as you can.** Small things can go a long way in helping them through a transition such as how packing will be handled or which day of the week the move will happen.

After the child leaves:

- **Offer ongoing support to the child or the new foster parent if there is still a good relationship,** such as respite, babysitting, or answering questions as they pop up, etc.
- **Consider seeking additional support for yourself** such as attending support groups, therapy, or spending time with family and friends. It's good to vent and process with others.

- **Try to find some related trainings to improve or enhance your parenting skills** in case a similar situation comes up in the future.
- **Consider modifying who you will accept during placement calls.** Of course, there will always be a leap of faith, but you may want to go back to your list of questions and make changes based on this experience.
- **You may want to get back into it more slowly.** Take a break, fill your cup, or potentially offer respite services as a step down from traditional fostering.

Still struggling?

An extended break may be really restorative to you and your family. This could be six to twelve months off from foster care, and then a restart after you've had a chance to tend to your mental and physical health and fully reset.

Ultimately, you may decide it's best to close your home. Foster parenting is not easy, and it can take a toll on families. It's really healthy to acknowledge what you can and can't do.

Whatever you decide, I hope that you can find some peace in your heart and find a path forward in a way that makes sense for you and your family.

15
Leaving Foster Care

TL;DR: Foster parents can support kids through reunification, transitions, and aging out of foster care by listening to and addressing their concerns, allowing for as much choice and control as possible. Being organized and advocating for information and transition support can go a long way for youth.

Big Changes in a Foster Home

Life events occur in many families: moving homes, changing schools, or a new baby coming soon. Families process and support their kids through changes. Parents have to adapt themselves to these changes while also remaining calm, strong, and steady for their children as they move through the seasons of change. In foster homes, changes are at the core of how foster care works and operates. Kids enter foster care (a traumatic experience), and then kids eventually exit foster care (which can come with loss, fear, joy, relief, and beyond). When kids leave a home, it impacts not just the child leaving, but everyone in the home, their relatives, and beyond.

In this chapter, you'll find information about the ways that kids exit foster care: reunification with parents, permanency with relatives or foster parents, or eventually aging out.

Transition Basics from the Community

Don't promise anything until you know it's certain.

It's important you don't promise a child anything until you know it is certain. Things can change quickly, and foster parents may not be privy to what is happening behind the scenes with the case, so transitions can feel sudden. For some kids, though, you can offer a preview of what may be happening, and that can be helpful for youth who want to be involved in what is going on. 💬 "If the judge allows, the next step is usually overnight visits with your mom before you return home." "The judge will decide what's next for you. They may choose to wait a little longer, or they may decide that they want you to move to your grandma's house."

Advocate for a transition plan.

Some kids, especially those who have been in foster care for some time, can really benefit from having a transition plan, which typically refers to a visit plan that increases time with their parents gradually before kids fully move home. It may start with unsupervised visits, overnight or weekend visits, and in some places, they may even do a trial home visit, where they have overnight visits for a longer time with check-ins from the worker. These plans help give kids time to adjust and get closure from living with you. If a transition plan is taking place, you can create a visual calendar so kids can keep track of when they are going home.

Offer as much choice and control as possible.

These small moments of choice and control can help kids feel more settled in what is happening. This could be choice of what to pack for overnights, what to listen to in the car, or the restaurant for your last dinner together, etc.

Get organized early.

It can take a little time to get everything organized, so start this early. This includes cleaning and packing the child's items, making sure all of the paperwork is updated, making sure everyone on the team has been informed, etc. If everything is buttoned up and ready to go, you can focus your final moments on the child and their needs.

Don't forget the permanent kids in the home.

They need what you need: understanding of the process, room and time to process the change, and support in sadness and grief. You can read books like *The Invisible String*, by Patrice Karst, or other kids' books about sadness and loss to open the door to these conversations.

Tools to Help

- ☐ **Toy houses and figurines:** Using playhouses and figurines can be a good way to explain transition plans to little kids.
- ☐ **Extra bins, duffel bags, and suitcases:** Grab some extra packing supplies when you see them on sale. If the child has been with you for a while, you may be surprised how much they have accumulated while with you!
- ☐ **Visual calendar:** A visual calendar can be a great way to show when visits, overnights, and the last day will be.

Saying Goodbye

What to Pack

Before you pack, check with the parent(s) to make sure they want everything returned and if they have space for everything. For example, they may not want outgrown clothing or have space to store a bike. Don't forget to pack:

- ☐ Clothing, shoes, accessories (don't forget to check the laundry!)
- ☐ Toiletries or self-care items
- ☐ Stuffed animals, comfort items, blankies
- ☐ Outgrown but still wearable clothing and shoes (parents may want these items for another sibling or relative)
- ☐ Items given as a gift to the child
- ☐ Any items the child has purchased with their own money
- ☐ Past schoolwork, current school projects, school supplies or tech for school
- ☐ Any money the child has saved while they've been with you
- ☐ Medications and copies of the prescription and medical insurance cards
- ☐ Full list of contacts of anyone who is continuing services. If it makes sense, you can include the contact info of the babysitters you've used
- ☐ Lifebook and a digital copy of photos

> Typically large furniture items that are used for all kids in the home are not returned (such as beds, car seats, or strollers). If the parent needs these types of items, it's up to you to decide to provide them, or you can offer to help crowdsource. There may also be a local nonprofit that can help!

The Last Goodbye

Kids may have a variety of complex feelings when returning home. They may be bouncing off the walls, excited to get back home. They may be worried and unsure if things will actually be different for them. They may feel sad about leaving you. More often than not, it is a combination of feelings, and they likely don't have the words or ability to express or understand them all. For little ones, perhaps they don't fully understand what is going on. In this final moment:

- **Match the kid's tone.** For example, if they are excited and happy, you can share in this celebration. If they are crying and not wanting to leave, you can offer a compassionate and encouraging goodbye.

> Try to avoid taking up too much space in this moment with your own tears and sadness. They may misinterpret your tears for worry or fear, or they may not understand why you are crying and think they have done something wrong.

- **Try to say what you need to say the day before.** The last moments can move quickly, and parents are eager to start this next chapter. It's great to get closure and tell the child how proud you are of them, but it may make sense to have these conversations the day before. That way, in the moments of goodbye, you don't have to suddenly remember everything, and you can focus on supporting the child with their parent(s) in this moment.

> If you don't have any advance notice about reunification, keep the goodbye simple with the goal of closure. "It has been an honor caring for you. You are going to do great things in life, and I will always remember and cherish our time together." Don't make promises about contact in the future, unless it has been agreed to ahead of time with their parent(s).

- **Offer encouragement to the parent(s), and if you are open to continuing to help, tell them.** This is a big moment for their parent(s). Reunification is not easy, and this has likely been a traumatic experience for them. Depending on your relationship, you can offer encouraging words, and you can let them know that you are open to babysitting or providing respite in the future.

Saying goodbye to a child can be sad, but you'd be surprised how inspiring, joyful, and fulfilling it can be, as well. You and your family helped a child through one of the hardest periods of their life, and now you get to see them reunite with their family. That is special. It will give you all the feels, so try to take everything in to remember this moment; it's likely one of the reasons you wanted to become a foster parent in the first place.

When a Youth Doesn't Want to Return Home

As a foster parent, you are working alongside families to support reunification, while also balancing advocating for the child and their concerns and needs. The goal of foster care is reunification, but when kids tell us about unsafe plans (like running away to escape reunification), it can be a nuanced situation that takes care and consideration.

- Listen and take them seriously.
- Allow them to vent without judgment.
- Write down their concerns so they can visually see that you are listening and prioritizing them.
- Ask them if they want to meet with their attorney, CASA, or GAL, or if they want to write a letter to the judge about their concerns. Know the policies in your state/county. In some areas, youth of a certain age can have a voice in the decision-making and have a formal opportunity to express their concerns and dictate what happens to them.
- Alert the worker and the therapist about expressed concerns (with the youth's permission). The child may benefit from working through their experiences with the therapist. You can ask if it makes sense for the therapist to meet with the parent(s) and child in a group session.
- Ask the worker about a slower transition plan. This can help the youth see firsthand and trust that circumstances have changed (or allow time for them to voice concerns that are still present).
- Make sure the youth knows where to go and who to talk to if there are problems after reunification or if they feel like running away. Provide brochures for youth shelters, or encourage them to put the runaway hotline/text line in their phone. Explain who they can go to if there is a problem, like their teacher, school counselor, or doctor.

Ways to Remember Kids Who Were in Your Home

I'm a nostalgic person, and finding ways to remember kids has been incredibly helpful to process the loss. Finding tangible ways to remember kids can also be supportive to your permanent children in the home. They formed bonds with their foster siblings and may also be feeling sadness, loss, or worry.

- Create a collage/photo book for each child
- Plant a new perennial flower that you can enjoy each year
- Create a Christmas ornament with their photo
- Personalize home items like mugs, calendars, pillows, etc., with the kids' names or pictures
- Order personalized jewelry with each child's birthstone or initial
- Work with your permanent children to create wall art or an ongoing project that symbolizes the children who have come through the home. An example: Use a wall decal or create a tree painting, and as each child moves in, you can add a leaf with their name.

After a Child Leaves Your Home

- **Decide if you will be holding your home for the child.** Some foster parents decide to keep a bed available for that child for a period of time while reunification is still new, in case the child has to return back to foster care. If you are doing this, you should tell the worker. Let them know that you have a bed available for them for the next few weeks, if something should change and the child needs to come back to your home. Of course, the hope is that reunification is safe and successful, so this isn't a requirement of foster parents. I share it in case it's something you wish to do.

- **Decide if you will be putting your home on hold for all placements.** Some foster parents also put their home on hold to process, reflect, grieve, and reset. The feelings of grief or ambiguous loss are real considerations for foster parents. Breaks can be restorative and necessary. These breaks can also be a good time to catch up on needed trainings.
- **Restock supplies** as needed. Especially if you are an emergency foster care provider, check in on the first-night supplies and make sure you are good to go again!
- **Reorganize bins of toys, clothing, etc.,** that didn't go home with the child. Relabel bins as needed and tidy/reorganize your playroom so that it is fresh and ready for the next kid.
- **Update bedrooms based on your experiences,** and give them a deep clean. My foster care bedroom took many forms as I learned what kids *really* need.
- **Put together the next welcome kit** so you are ready to go. Update the welcome binder based on things you've learned or changed along the way.
- **Take down the posted paperwork** related to the last child.
- **Purchase a new lifebook** or photo album.
- **Take this opportunity to reconnect with your partner** and permanent children, and see friends and family during this time of transition.
- **Attend a support group** or connect with your therapist to help you

cope with this change and loss. Connect with your permanent children in the home and see if they need support too. 💬 Connect, validate, and reassure: "I feel sad too, but this sad feeling won't always be there." "You aren't alone in your sadness. It's okay to feel sad. I'm here to be with you through this."

- **Reconnect with all members of the home** to make sure they all want to say yes again. Be careful not to pressure them, and create a safe place for your permanent children to share their genuine wishes or concerns.
- **Restock your freezer** with meals that can easily be reheated during the stressful first month with a new placement.
- **Sleep!**

Preparing a Child for TPR and Beyond

While the hope is that circumstances will improve for the child's parent(s), it isn't always possible. The court may decide that reunification is no longer in the child's best interests, and they may decide on termination of parental rights (TPR). This ends the legal relationship between the parent(s) and the child, and the child will not return home.

TPR can be complex. Some kids have a complicated mix of feelings about it. Relief and grief. Hope and sadness. They may not know how to feel. They may look to you for comfort.

Talking to the Child

Like many hard conversations in foster care, this one will probably unfold over time. Here are some examples of what you can say, from the beginning of their stay with you until TPR and permanency:

AT THE BEGINNING:

"I will be taking care of you while your parents aren't able."

"I hope you can return home soon."

AS YOU START TO HEAR ABOUT TPR POSSIBLY HAPPENING:

"Court is coming up. Some things may be changing. For now, you are staying with us."

"We don't know what will happen next, but right now, we are taking care of you."

AS PERMANENT CAREGIVERS ARE BEING CONSIDERED:

"I have an update for you. You are going to start spending time with your grandmother."

"Next week, you are going to spend the night with your grandmother."

WHEN PLANS HAVE BEEN FINALIZED:

"At the end of the month, you will be moving in with your grandmother. The court has decided that is the best place for you to live."

"You won't be returning home to your parent(s). You will live with your grandparents."

For younger kids, the book *Families Change*, written by Julie Nelson and illustrated by Mary Gallagher, is written for kids going through TPR. It can help you open the door for these conversations.

Considerations for these conversations:

- Some kids don't do well with "maybe," and it can make more sense to not share details until you know what is happening for certain, while other kids want to know what is happening and want to contribute along the way. And in some places, youth participate in these court hearings.
- It can be helpful to point out what *won't* be changing, to offer a point of stability as they process the changes around them.
- Staying neutral and being aware of your body language are important during these moments. You don't want your feelings about the situation getting in the way of them expressing theirs. For example, you might be planning to adopt them and have some excitement that foster care is ending, but the child may feel hesitant or really scared. They may not feel comfortable expressing their true feelings if they see that you're excited.
- The child's therapist can help you identify the best ways to communicate these changes based on their therapeutic needs.

Helping a Youth as They Age Out of Foster Care

Kids who don't return home and do not find permanency will age out of foster care. Foster parents have an incredible opportunity to support youth during this transition.

Information and Documents

This is incredibly important. Please help track down workers, and visit local government offices with the youth to help them collect the following:

- ☐ Proof of Dependency or Proof of Wardship letter—this document in particular is very important to access services and funding reserved for former foster youth later in life. This can be incredibly difficult to get once the youth loses direct contact with the worker.
- ☐ Case files and court documents—anything is better than nothing
- ☐ Social Security number and card
- ☐ Original birth certificate
- ☐ Driver's license
- ☐ Passport
- ☐ School records and diploma
- ☐ Health insurance card
- ☐ Credit report
- ☐ Immigration or citizenship documents, if applicable
- ☐ Copy of or access to immunization and health records
- ☐ Photos (you can help by reaching out to past workers and foster parents to ask for photos)
- ☐ A family tree, with full names and contact information when possible. If you have cultural or medical information about family members, include this too!

> Be sure to help the youth scan these documents and make copies of everything! This is a great opportunity to teach them about how to keep documents organized digitally. If you are open to it, ask them if they want you to keep a copy of anything for them.

School

For youth who have moved schools several times, they may be missing credits or not have good enough grades to graduate. There's a lot foster parents can do, alongside their CASA, worker, and teachers, to help them graduate, such as looking into options for credit recovery or requesting partial credit for work completed.

From there, you can help them find a college, technical school, or job to take them to the next phase of life. Depending on where you live, the youth may be able to get reduced or free tuition or other support (e.g., meals, books, housing, bus passes) because they spent time in foster care.

When touring or considering a college, ask about:

- Safety procedures for the campus and in the dorm
- Living options, including what is available during holidays and breaks
- Current or former foster youth support services, such as peer connections, mental health support, or academic services
- Disability services and accommodations
- Job opportunities on campus

Careers

There is so much that foster parents can do to help youth get their first job and work in their preferred field.

- Work with youth to identify areas of interest and strengths. Teach them about the different career paths and job opportunities that match. Their teachers or school counselor may also have insights into what careers they may thrive in.

- Help them write their résumé and cover letter and teach them about the online tools that exist to find job postings.
- Take them shopping to find interview outfits and work clothing.
- Be a reference for them, or write a letter of recommendation. Ask your friends and family to do the same.
- Ask your friends, family, and professional network if they know of any job openings or networking events. Help connect the youth to your community, and give advice on how to effectively network.
- Reach out to local nonprofits that support transition-age youth and former foster youth to understand what resources and supports exist. Many of these organizations can help connect them with mentorship and job training.

Skills for Adulthood

There's a lot to learn about being an adult. They won't learn everything overnight, but foster parents play a vital role in helping youth:

- Learn how to do laundry and keep their home clean
- Manage their finances, bank accounts, credit cards; avoid scams; maintain a good credit score; file taxes
- Put together a shopping list, use basic kitchen skills, understand food safety standards
- Learn how to drive and obtain their license and registration
- Understand the medical system, including navigating medical insurance claims, scheduling doctor's appointments, and prescription management
- Register to vote, and submit a mail-in ballot or vote in person

- Navigate various related systems, such as food stamps or food pantries, state disability programs, housing programs, courts, etc.
- Know what to do in an emergency (whether that emergency has to do with illness, an accident, mental health, legal trouble, etc.). Consider creating an emergency contact list with them and helping them put it in their phone. Include any adults who could be supportive plus specialized hotlines based on their needs.

Information for You

Foster care stipends will end when the youth ages out of foster care. This typically happens from age eighteen to twenty-one years old depending on your area, and there are even programs that can extend longer. You may not be able to afford to care for them without the reimbursement. If you know that you won't be able to support them financially into adulthood, please make a plan early so they have stable housing and their basic needs will continue to be met. Look for transition-age youth programs in your county, and the worker should also be able to connect them with programs. Young people need positive and supportive adults in their life, so even if they can't live with you, please consider being there for them through this transitional part of their life.

Additionally, once the youth turns eighteen, if they are remaining in your home, there's likely additional paperwork they need to complete in order for you to keep fostering other children. If they have a criminal record, there's a chance you won't be able to foster children with them in the home. Talk to the worker early if you have other kids in the home who could be impacted.

All that is to say: I hope you continue to be a supportive adult and mentor in their life. We aren't meant to do life alone. Even if they are pushing you away and ready to leave foster care behind, make sure they have your number, and assure them you will always take their call.

Part 3

Navigating Systems and Advocacy Outside the Home

I signed up to be a foster parent to help a *child*...

...After fostering my first child, I realized what I signed up to do was help *families*.

16

Working with the Professional Team

TL;DR: Working with the professional team is important, and foster parents will need to be proactive, organized, and use purposeful communication strategies to advocate and work effectively with the worker, advocates, school professionals, therapists, and beyond.

Parenting Alongside a Team of Professionals

Families today work closely with their child's teachers and doctors to make sure their kids are growing and developing appropriately. They may work with a therapist during hard seasons. Families with children with special needs often have several professionals in their life who meet with the child frequently and also support the family. In foster homes, similar things are taking place. In addition to those professionals, foster parents also have government officials who visit the home to closely monitor their parenting practices and how the child is doing. On top of all that, there are policies, procedures, and red tape baked into the foster care system that often cause delays and miscommunications.

The professionals' expertise guides foster parents and the rest of the team in finding the best ways to support the child. They can be instrumental in the child's life, but there can also be challenges in working with team members. They often have high caseloads and need to work within the policies, procedures, and red tape that cause inefficiencies within the system. Foster parents, along with the professional team, play an important role in making sure the child in their care doesn't fall through the deep cracks of the child welfare system.

The professional team may include:

- Worker (agency worker, county worker, and their supervisors)—sometimes they are social workers; sometimes they have different credentials
- Advocate (attorney, GAL, or CASA)
- Mental health team (therapist, behaviorist, in-home mental health team, etc.)
- Medical team (pediatrician, psychiatrist, nurse, specialists, dietitian, etc.)
- Developmental team (occupational therapist, speech therapist, physical therapist, child development specialist, feeding therapist, etc.)
- School staff (teachers, principal, special education teachers and staff, coaches, counselors, foster child liaisons, etc.)

The Basics of Working with the Team

Understanding how to cultivate a professional relationship with the entire team is important as you work through and support difficult moments in foster care. These relationships may also come with some challenges of their own, such as poor communication, miscommunications, turnover, or not respecting boundaries. Foster parents must be able to work with a variety of personalities and styles to effectively advocate for the child in their care.

When starting a new relationship, ask their communication preferences.

Review how they wish to be contacted for nonurgent and urgent matters. Each person will want to get general updates on the child differently too. For example, the worker may want an email recap each week, while the attorney may send their assistant to your home to collect all the info before court. You should also consider sharing *your* communication preferences, such as who is the point person in the home, or what email and phone number they should use.

Get everything in writing.

It can be a little annoying to follow up with texts and emails, but your future self will thank you! Having written records of when you request services, referrals, and paperwork and report incidents, etc., can help in your advocacy efforts. (More on that in chapter 19.)

Diversify your contacts.

Try to get to know all members of the professional team, including their supervisors. That way, if you don't hear back from one person, you have other people you can contact who may be able to help you. In some places, there are foster parent helplines you can call to get general information.

Loop in others, if needed.

When you haven't heard back from someone, it can be helpful to include others in the emails you send. First, make sure you are giving people a sufficient amount of time to respond and are following their preferred communication style. If the matter is urgent or of high importance, and you haven't heard back, loop in other team members or their supervisor on the follow-up email. Continue to go up the chain of command until you hear back.

Honor boundaries.

If you don't hold your own boundaries, no one will. If you have constraints in your schedule, or if you know you aren't able to accommodate something (like supervising visits or accepting a baby sibling), it's important to make the boundaries known. And with that, it's also important you respect the professional's boundaries, as well as be respectful of the confines of their specific role. Each member of the professional team is often limited in scope of what they can and cannot do. Everyone must be flexible and have grace for each other's needs, while balancing your personal needs. You don't want to burn out.

A NOTE OF CAUTION FROM ANOTHER FOSTER PARENT

"We didn't know how to advocate for ourselves and ended up getting burnt out by being so flexible with every last-minute (but not emergent or required/needed for kiddos) request made by CPS, CASA, or even our own agency."

Prioritize and focus requests.

You may get a faster response if you simplify your requests and prioritize needs. For example, if the child needs referrals for multiple things, just ask for one at a time. When you have a home visit or team meeting, you can discuss all needs.

Kindness goes a long way.

Showing compassion for everyone's limits and needs can be a helpful tone to set when resolving conflicts or discussing hard topics. It is possible to be firm and kind, but for me this took some practice. You can show kindness by respecting vacation time, scheduling your emails to send during work hours, and writing a positive email to their supervisor.

Refocus on the kids.

Re-centering the conversation on the kids' needs and what is best for the kids can be a helpful way to work through complex situations. Instead of using "I" statements, try refocusing on the *child* and *their* needs.

Use strength-based language.

Focus on the positive attributes and what the child *can do well*, rather than using language that focuses on the problems (e.g., "energetic" rather than "can't sit still" or "determined" rather than "defiant"). Certain labels can also be harmful and lasting for youth (such as "flight risk" or "aggressive"). The goal isn't to tiptoe around a child's needs, but when you can start from a place of strength and positivity as you describe the child, it can also help others on the team consider these things too. So much progress can be made when we use a child's strengths as part of their treatment. Additionally, foster parents' words make it into kids' case files, which they can look through once they've grown up. Your words will still be there, and it matters how you describe the kids you have cared for.

For example, you could share, "Riley is energetic, and likes to move around and climb on many things. They could benefit from flexible seating in the classroom, movement breaks, and after-school sports activities (they are especially great at soccer!). They have a determined spirit, and do best when given choice and control over their activities. They do well sharing their opinions and preferences with adults and use strong language when doing so. They could benefit from therapy to help them learn how to be more flexible and respectful during disagreements, and to help them find ways to regulate their emotions in a safe way. Without this help, there are safety risks, and they may be at risk of suspension. Intervention is needed as soon as possible.

Examples of words you can use:

- Authentic
- Bold
- Brave
- Calm
- Caring
- Charismatic
- Compassionate
- Competitive
- Confident
- Creative
- Detail-oriented
- Determined
- Direct
- Empathetic
- Energetic
- Expressive
- Focused
- Friendly
- Funny
- Good friend
- Helpful
- Imaginative
- Inspiring
- Kind
- Leader
- Mindful
- Observant
- Organized
- Passionate
- Persistent
- Playful
- Reliable
- Silly
- Smart
- Strong
- Tech savvy
- Thoughtful
- Unique

If the child's needs are being *severely underserved* by the professionals in their life, check out chapter 19 for ideas to take your advocacy to the next level.

Team Meetings

In many places, there are formal team meetings where you get together with the worker and other professionals who are working with the child. Usually, it follows a preset agenda that reviews the child's strengths, areas of need, and goals. The child and the parent(s) may also be at this meeting.

Before the meeting:

- Understand the type of team meeting and its purpose. These meetings may change as the case progresses. It's good to be prepared.
- Write down the child's and parents' strengths, which you can share during the meeting. Often this part gets rushed, and it may be hard to think of something on the spot (at least, it is for me!). I like to write it down, so I make sure I include this information in the meeting. The notes may be included in the child's case file or even shared in court, so you want to make sure you are intentional with your word choices to uplift the kids and their parent(s).
- Also, write down any questions you may have for the team, and rank them according to priority, as there may not be time to ask everything. Connect with the youth, and see if they want to write down any questions or concerns as well.

During the meeting:

- Use language that is respectful and honors the parent(s) like "your child" and "mom" rather than ✖ "bio mom."
- Take notes, even if there is a notetaker assigned to the meeting, in case details are missed on the final documents.
- Make space in the conversation for the child to speak. Consider giving them an opportunity to share or answer the question first, before you.
- If the child is present, make sure you are building them up and using positive language, even when discussing harder subjects. For example: "Charlie has so much potential at school. I'd love some support at IEP meetings to help ensure he's getting everything he needs to succeed," or "Charlie is working really hard on expressing himself safely. I'd love additional support from a therapeutic team to come up with a safety plan to further help and build on his efforts."
- As the meeting ends, align on when the next meeting will happen.

After the meeting:

- Request a copy of the notes or anything you signed.
- If there is a next step from the meeting, follow up by email with an overview of what you will be working on.

What to bring to appointments and meetings:

- ☐ Snacks and drinks for the kids (and for you!)
- ☐ Diaper bag and everything needed for infant care

- ☐ Comfort item(s)
- ☐ Activities for the child—even if you meet at the department's office, don't assume it will be in a room with toys. You may end up in a room with just a big conference table or a circle of chairs.
- ☐ Kids' medication or medical devices, etc. Assume the meeting will go long, so bring what they will need.
- ☐ Folder of only the most important information and any papers you need to hand off to another person at the meeting. If parents will be there, you could bring recent crafts or photos to share.
- ☐ A laptop can be helpful if it's an in-depth meeting where you need to refer to emails or specific paperwork
- ☐ Beverage—this is a personal one, but I'm including it! I like to take small sips of a bubbly water or a hot tea or coffee to help regulate myself during a hard meeting or to force a pause before I interject or respond.
- ☐ Notebook and writing tools for taking notes
- ☐ Calendar or planner for scheduling or referencing past appointments

School Considerations

Teachers and school staff can be some of the most important people in a child's life. They might have been the person to call the child abuse hotline originally and open up the investigation. For some kids, their teacher and their classroom was their only safe place.

School can also be the most challenging part of a child's life. They may be severely behind academically from moving from school to school or not attending for long periods of time. They may not have strong friendships at school or be a victim of bullying. They may be displaying trauma responses at school that can create unsafe situations. They may be labeled as the “bad” kid and find themselves getting blamed and punished for *everything*. As you support through it all, consider:

Privacy Needs

You can advocate for kids without sharing sensitive information about their history. Additionally, some youth do not want teachers or peers at school knowing they are in foster care. You can always share something general like, 💬 “Chelsea is going through some hard things in her personal life. I'd love to talk about some support she may need.” The worker can help guide on what should and shouldn't be shared, as well as who holds educational rights for the youth. Make sure you explain to the youth who is required to know about their foster care status.

Parents

It can be helpful (and sometimes required) for parents to be involved in school communications, conferences, IEP meetings, and beyond. Their involvement in their child's schooling can help them demonstrate their parenting abilities, and it also helps them stay up-to-date with their child. If parents aren't involved directly at the school, you can still keep them updated by sending homework, projects, and books with the youth to visits to work on with their parent(s). Try to scan important schoolwork ahead of a visit in case it gets lost or left at the facility.

Communication

Most teachers want to do what they can to help kids in care, and foster parents can set them up for success by communicating strengths, interests, motivators, triggers, and ways to help them regulate. 💬 “June is going through some difficult family changes, so she may be sensitive to family-based school projects. Any alternative projects would be appreciated." Don't assume that they have been given any background info about the child and their family circumstances. A lot of the time, teachers are not informed by their school about the child's foster care status.

Accommodations, Supports, and Requests

Having the appropriate supports in place at school will have a big impact on the child's day-to-day success. Some kids may qualify for an IEP or 504 plan. In addition to those formal supports, there are other things you can request. I asked the community what types of things helped their kids in school, and these are some of what was shared:

Trauma-conscious supports:

- Calming spaces in the classroom for kids to take a break, if needed (classroom library, tent, calming zone, sensory supports, etc.)
- Warning or heads-up to child and foster parent about active shooter drills, fire drills, etc., foreshadowing when these will happen, checking in with student after the drill
- Notifying foster parent and youth when there will be a sub (if possible)
- Notifying foster parent about specific movies being shown in class
- Sessions or check-ins with school counselors or social workers
- Not forcing "close your eyes" activities or not making the room completely dark
- Allowing kids to use the restroom at any time
- If the child is being called to the office, writing why on the slip (e.g., "You are being asked to go to the office to take your medicine" is better than ✘ "Go to the office, they need you for something.")

- Social groups, friendship groups, grief groups, support groups for students
- Printed and posted schedules
- Eating with a small group or in a quiet area during lunchtime
- Transition plans for coming back to school after long periods of school refusal or not attending school
- Providing as much control as possible to the youth throughout the day
- School staff being supportive about mental health days
- Being open to foster parents volunteering in the classroom or on field trips
- Creating and following safety plans, and sharing them broadly with all adults who support the youth throughout the day

Classwork and homework:

- Using inclusive language like "caregiver," "grown-up," or "adult," and portraying different types of families in books and activities
- Clear communication to foster parents about what work is required vs. optional (not graded)
- Getting an extra copy of homework or projects (or the ability to email a digital copy to the foster parent to reprint at home if the item goes missing or is left at a visit)
- Offering for the child to make two Mother's Day and two Father's Day gifts, or allowing the child to opt out entirely
- Deadline extensions or additional time for homework or projects
- Modifying family tree, "all about me," or baby picture projects to be optional, or allowing all kids to create them for a historical/famous person instead (it's important youth in care aren't being singled out)

- Not punishing kids for missing class due to court, visits, mental health days, etc.
- Not publicly shaming or calling out kids for late assignments or not turning in homework
- Multiple options for credit recovery or partial credit for work completed

Documentation

- Written documentation about when they have to visit the nurse (even for scrapes)
- Written documentation about behavioral or emotional needs or incidents
- Sending home permission slips early
- A checkout system, making sure child leaves with the approved people

Supports Outside of School

Foster parents have an opportunity to help get kids caught up at school and ensure their education continues while in foster care.

- Sign up for all of the school robocalls, PTA emails, online homework portals, teacher communication apps, and Facebook groups to stay connected and in the know.
- Create a dedicated homework station for kids to use. It doesn't have to be fancy or a big space, but having a place where kids do their work can help make it part of the routine. It's a place to organize their papers, keep school supplies, and do their work independently or with your help. Collaborate with the youth on the setup to get their buy-in.

- Ask the teacher what the top priority is for the youth if they are struggling in multiple areas. Follow the teacher's recommendations.
- For homework help, there may be YouTube videos you can play to help the youth (and you!) learn. Some districts or local libraries may have free homework help too.
- Get creative to help them learn in different ways and to stay on track. For example, if the youth is given a required reading in school but is several grade levels behind in reading, you can supplement their reading with listening to chapters in audiobook form, or you can read and point to the words. Their teacher likely has many helpful ideas, so ask!
- Some youth may need tutoring or educational therapy, which can provide more individualized approaches. You can ask the worker or their advocate for additional funding to pay for this service.
- Don't forget sports, music, and extracurriculars. For some youth, these activities can play an important role in their social and emotional development. They also introduce youth to other adult role models and mentors, and enhance normalcy.

Working with the team can feel like a whole other full-time job on its own, especially when you have a sibling group or you are caring for youth that need a variety of services. Each professional brings unique skills and expertise, along with their own set of roadblocks and constraints. With clear communication and organization, you can be an important part of making sure the child doesn't slip through the cracks. Thank you for doing the work!

17

Working with Parents

TL;DR: Having a relationship with the child's parent(s) builds over time. Use friendly, professional communication and conflict resolution skills to work through disagreements. Understand that parents are also going through a time of crisis, so patience and compassion, even during stressful times like a false allegation, are important for a safe and trusting relationship.

Group Parenting

Families are diverse—some kids have a single parent or a two-parent household, or perhaps their parents are divorced and they move back and forth between homes. This can cause unique co-parenting dynamics that families have to work through. Foster families are also diverse, and they also have to consider parenting guidelines that are dictated by the government, parents' requests and differing parenting methods, and other biological family that may or may not be involved in their day-to-day life. On top of that, siblings may be separated into different foster homes, which can affect their dynamic and relationship.

A FOSTER PARENT SHARED THIS REFLECTION

"Looking back, I think the amount of caution I had regarding first families [parents] wasn't inappropriate, but now that I've expanded my perspective on cultivating those relationships while maintaining healthy boundaries, I have become more open and engaging with first families [parents]."

Relationship-Building Basics from the Community

Relationships with parents can take many forms. Some may be open to working together and eager to co-parent, while others may prefer not to engage with you. Regardless of how the parent responds, consider the things *you* can control. You can control how you interact, include the parent(s), and honor the child's desires. The parent is going through a crisis, and so they may or may not be ready or able to engage with you or have active involvement with their child.

Start the relationship with an icebreaker meeting or comfort call.

Foster parents and parents meet in a variety of ways. It may be in a formal icebreaker meeting, or it may be less formal like a phone call or meeting them at a visit. This first meeting is a good time to introduce yourself and ask some questions about their child. There will be so much you want to learn about their child, but you may need to ask these questions over a few conversations. For these first interactions:

- Set a friendly, professional tone.
- Introduce your role and reiterate that you are there to support and care for their child until they can go back home.
- Share about your home, who lives there, and what their bedroom is like.
- Share your experience caring for kids this age to help instill confidence, but leave room for their input to show you value their collaboration. 💬 "Usually for this age-group, we do bath, books, and then bedtime around seven p.m. I know keeping a consistent schedule is so important. Does that align with how things happen in your home?" or "I use free and clear detergent for kids in our home. Do you find that works okay for your kid's skin? I know many kids have sensitivities."
- Ask them questions about their kids:
  - » Favorite foods, TV shows, characters, books, songs, etc.
  - » Medical needs: 💬 "I saw in the notes from the worker that your daughter is allergic to peanuts. Is there anything else she is allergic to, or does she have any other medical needs?" Make sure they know you are reading the documents and taking this seriously, and it's also good to confirm details.
  - » Routines for naps, feeding, or bedtime
  - » Fears, worries, or concerns, and how to comfort them when they are upset or sick
  - » Friend circle, dating partner, anything you should be aware of as it relates to peers

 - » Sports, extracurriculars, hobbies
 - » Strengths and areas of need in school
 - » Cultural or family traditions, especially as you approach different holidays

- Align on what is shared with younger children about where their parents are (e.g., "Mommy is getting help," "Mommy is learning about being a mom"). You don't want to lie to children, but it's also important to use age-appropriate language.
- You can reiterate how you hope to work together and that they can talk to you if there's ever a concern:  "I know there may be questions or concerns that come up along the way. Please feel free to text or give me a call."

> Don't forget to ask for translation services if it would be helpful to communicate better with the parent(s).

Get the perspective of the youth in your care.

Check in with them to understand their needs or concerns related to their parent and visits. Kids may be upset that you are being kind to their parent(s) if their parent(s) harmed them. They may also feel loyalty to their parent(s) or struggle with split loyalty. It's good to explain your role and how you are required to engage with parents in a professional manner and follow court orders regarding their parent and relative visits. You can assure the child that you aren't replacing their parent(s) and that you are there to help care for them until they can go home.

Respect boundaries.

Not every parent will want to or be able to engage in a back-and-forth relationship. Sometimes, especially at the beginning, parents may need space to process, and you may need to gain their trust. Don't be pushy or take things personally. Just focus on providing consistent care for their children.

Communicate your boundaries.

You may have a parent who wants active engagement with you multiple times a day. At the beginning, they may feel scared and worried. You are a stranger who is caring for their child. It's natural for them to want to check in, ask questions, and ensure their child is okay. It may be helpful to acknowledge their needs and set up a communication plan. 💬 "I want to make sure you have all the information you need for your child. Let's set up an ongoing plan for us to communicate and share updates." Initially, it may make sense to share updates through the worker or a communication journal. Some families set up a shared photo drive online that the worker and parent have access to, or you can print photos to share at visits.

Build a relationship over time.

Just like the kids in your home, building a trusting relationship with their parent(s) can take time, and sometimes it may feel like two steps forward and one step back. This can happen if there are changes in case plans, visitation, or something happens in their personal life. I always tried to remind myself that they have also experienced trauma.

They may have experienced childhood abuse or neglect themselves.

They may have been in foster care.

They may be currently experiencing domestic violence or other traumatic life circumstances.

They may have limited resources.

They have needs that may not be met right now.

They may not have a village showing up for them.

I won't ever fully understand what they are going through.

Ways to take steps forward with parents and support the relationship over time:

- Acknowledge them during the holidays and Mother's and Father's Day
- Provide thoughtful, encouraging letters and sentiments. Make sure these are genuine and not performative. 💬 "You are such a great mother." "He is so happy when he's with you." "I hope they can return home soon." "You've raised an amazing kid—he is so funny and smart." "He gets his smarts from his mother!" "I noticed you spoke up in the meeting about his safety in the transport vehicle. Thank you so much for bringing that up. That's very worrying; I'm so glad you were checking on that."

> Note that some departments have limits on gifting to parents, as it can be seen as a bribe. For example, something as small as a potted succulent is sometimes allowed, and sometimes it's not, so ask!

- Try to facilitate "firsts" with parents. This can include the first time trying solid food, first piece of cake, or first time riding a bike. You can also bring a lock of hair from their first haircut or the first tooth they lose.
- Include parents in appointments and conferences.

Supporting reunification and beyond:

- As parents are approaching reunification, try to find daycare providers that are close to where the parent lives so that daycare can continue after the child returns home.
- For school-age kids, you can set up free school lunches so that service can hopefully continue after kids move home. Some districts have free breakfast and dinner programs, too, which can be supportive for some families with limited resources.
- If the child has special needs, there may be state disability programs they qualify for that can provide further support for the family after reunification, such as developmental services and respite care. You can spend time getting this set up, so it's one less thing the parent has to manage during the transitional period.
- During team meetings, if you feel the children should be returning home, you can voice this in clear language. "The unsupervised visits have been very smooth, and the children share they are excited to return home. I support reunification." If it makes sense, express this to the child's advocate.
- If you are open to supporting the parent(s) after reunification, such as babysitting or providing respite, it may help the team feel more comfortable with reunification, knowing that they have you as an added support system.

> Understand that some families don't want any contact with foster families after reunification. They may want to put it in their past and move on. They may be fearful about contacting anyone connected to child welfare. They may not feel connected to you. That's okay too.

- Connect with the worker and parent(s) about possible supplies the parent(s) may need for the kids to return home. You may be able to help crowdsource needed items or connect them with a foster closet that can help support these efforts.
- When a kid returns home, the parents are in control. This means that all contact must be approved by or go through the child's parent(s). It's really important that the foster parents respect their authority and maintain healthy boundaries.

REMEMBER, YOU ARE DOING IMPORTANT WORK. THIS COMMUNITY MEMBER REITERATES THIS SENTIMENT

"Extending love, kindness, empathy, and connection beyond the child in your home to their biological family and community not only honors that child but can have ripple effects for entire families and communities."

When Things Come Up

Conflict

It's common for parents and foster parents to have to work through miscommunications or disagreements in parenting methods. Remember:

- Always maintain professionalism.
- Learn from the worker what you can and can't do to support parents so you are prepared if things come up (for example, whether you are allowed to drive them to visits, give them needed items, etc.).
- Be open to new ideas and learning new ways to support their child.
- Collaborate on solutions.
- Stay focused on the child, and their needs and well-being.
- Stick with facts and observations, rather than opinions.
- Remind parents of your role and your obligation to inform the worker of concerns.
- Involve them in appointments, such as doctor or dentist appointments, so they can hear directly from professionals (they may be more receptive to feedback if it comes from the professional directly). If they can't attend these meetings, bring a medical summary or brochures, or a doctor's note for the parent(s) to review.
- Avoid surprises, and try to give a warning when you need to change something in the schedule.
- Reiterate agreed-upon boundaries "I appreciate your call. Just a reminder that I am unavailable from seven a.m. to five p.m. for work and school pickup and drop-off."
- Get the worker involved to help resolve issues if they persist, or call a team meeting to discuss things as an entire group.
- If things get tense or don't resolve quickly, it is okay to slow down or step back in building the relationship. Things change in foster care, and the fact that it is hard now doesn't mean it will always be like this.

Allegations

The allegation process exists to keep kids safe. If someone is concerned about the safety of the child in the foster home, an allegation may be made, and an investigation may be opened.

If you foster for a while, you may encounter a situation where a parent or child makes a false allegation against you, or a situation was misinterpreted by a well-meaning person or mandated reporter as possible abuse or neglect. These can be very stressful situations, because kids can be removed from your home, and for some people (like those who work with children), it can impact their job.

> Before I dive into some things you can do to prevent false allegations from occurring, I want to take a moment to pause and reflect. Parents or youth may feel helpless and desperate for control, or may have a lot of fears and worries. They see and hear stories about horrible foster parents, and maybe they have had firsthand experience. Sometimes, they may not understand the process. For example, a youth may accuse the foster parent of something to try to move in with a friend instead, but this just isn't how it works. Many professionals err on the side of caution and report to be safe or because they are required to do so because they are a mandated reporter. The investigative process is in place for an important reason: to keep kids safe. Try your best not to take it personally. I know that is easier said than done.

There are many things that foster parents can do to reduce the likelihood of an allegation and to help protect themselves if one does occur. This includes:

- Understanding all that is required of you as a foster parent. This means that you need to be familiar with your state's written directives for foster parents, the policies and procedures or foster parent handbook, the Foster Parent Bill of Rights, and investigation procedures. Also be familiar with the foster child's rights and your agency's policies and procedures.
- Ensuring your home is always compliant and you are following the safety rules outlined in your home inspection forms.
- Being sure the children are up-to-date on medical and dental appointments, and you are taking the children in for follow-up appointments when they are requested by the medical professional.
- Turning in all of your required monthly paperwork on time.
- Following the safety plan at all times (if the child has one).
- Keeping up with your required foster parent trainings.
- Documenting all intense behaviors and injuries (with photos).
- Keeping open communication with the parent(s) 💬 "Please let me know if you ever have a question about your child in my care."
- Taking feedback or concerns from parents seriously and compassionately. Consider asking for a family team meeting to address their concerns, to show you are taking them seriously and care about their input. It can also be helpful to have the rest of the professional team weigh in on plans.
- Involving the case manager in escalating disagreements with parents and kids in your home. 💬 "I'm going to loop in the worker to make sure all of your concerns are addressed."
- If you feel yourself getting burned out, asking for help! See chapter 14 for more information.
- Being open and honest with the worker about things you are

struggling with or if you feel you've made a mistake with a child or in your relationship with the parent(s). It's better to address it head-on.

- Keeping an open dialogue with the child. Ask them how things are going and for their input on house rules, meals, etc. Take their feedback seriously.

When Parents Aren't Visiting

Parents may not always be in a place in their lives where they are able to prioritize their children. The hope is that parents are able to engage in services and improve their circumstances so kids can safely return home as soon as possible, but there may be periods when parents are not visiting. It's important to help kids stay connected to their parent(s), extended family, and culture the best you can, so their identity doesn't get lost in the cracks of the system.

- Request from the worker or relatives photos of the family to put up in your home, or create a photo book with the youth.
- Have the child write a letter or draw a photo for their parent(s). Save it for when you see their parent(s) again.
- For kids with many questions, keep a question box for them to put questions in any time they have one that can't be answered. Open this box whenever you have new information and try to answer some of the open questions.
- Connect with relatives or community members to maintain cultural and religious connections.

Safety Concerns Related to Visits or Reunification

The goal and hope are for positive, safe visits and reunification with parents. There may be times where you witness safety concerns or the child reports a safety concern during a visit. When this occurs, foster parents can advocate for safety in a variety of ways:

- **Educate parents.** If you notice something that is a safety concern, try discussing it with the parent(s) in a compassionate, helpful manner. Consider typing up instructions, including notes and summaries from the child's doctor, using visuals or labels for how medical equipment works, or showing parents firsthand how to do things in a safer manner (like using a car seat). Your tone is important in these interactions. You don't want to seem demeaning. 💬 "I taped the medication timeline onto the box so that I can remember. I left it there in case you want to reference it too."
- **Focus on the facts and personal observations.** Sometimes you may hear things from people related to the family. If a relative tells you something that is of concern, you can let them know that it's important they share directly with the worker. You can let the worker know that they should connect with the relative about safety concerns, but try not to be the intermediary. The worker needs to understand firsthand what is going on.
- **If the child shares concerns with you, type up what they shared or empower them to share directly with the worker or advocate.** Document the details about what the child shares, and suggest they tell their worker, or you can help them talk to their worker too. However, it's important to remember that you are a mandated

reporter. Make sure you are following protocols for when you need to report incidents to the child abuse hotline.

- **Get help with exchanges.** If there are notable concerns between you and the parent(s) during visit drop-offs or pickups, you can request transportation assistance for the visits or have the worker walk the kids to and from the car. Hopefully this is a temporary support, and the interactions can be improved over time.
- **Advocate for a transition plan.** Transition plans give parents an opportunity to get ready for their kids to return home and demonstrate their abilities to care for their children. In some states, judges may order extended or trial home visits that last several weeks or months. This is an opportunity for workers to continue to support the parent(s) with their children in their home before reunification is finalized. In some places, foster parents may hold space in their home during this extended visit in case kids need to return to them.

Being a foster parent isn't just about caring for a child. You are standing in the gap for an entire family. It is normal to feel unsure or for these types of relationships to feel unnatural at first. My best advice is to take it slow and follow the lead of both the child and their parent(s). These relationships aren't built quickly. But they are worth your time.

18
Supporting Parent Visits

TL;DR: Parent visits are important to keep bonds strong, as well as for parents to demonstrate their parenting skills. Foster parents can help set kids and parents up for success through clear communication, and having routines and backup plans.

Visiting with Family in Foster Care

Generally speaking, kids may visit with different family members, have to move back and forth between houses if their parents are divorced, or spend extended time with relatives. In these situations, parents typically will help kids transition to and from these visits and tune in closely to their needs or worries. This happens in foster care too. Foster parents play an important role in these transitions and should listen to children's concerns. However, neglect, abuse, and trauma add a nuanced layer to these visits, on top of the oversight of the government dictating specifics and monitoring interactions closely. In some situations, parents are not able to reliably show up at each visit or have stretches where they are not visiting at all, which can cause sadness or worry for their children.

Visits (also known as family time) are complex, ever-changing, and very important for reunification. Visits help keep a connection between the parent(s) and their child, and they are also important for parents to show the workers that they can safely care for their children.

Visit Basics from the Community

Get all the logistical details figured out and in writing.

If you discuss these details in a meeting or over the phone, you can reiterate what was agreed to in a follow-up email.

- Is it monitored or unmonitored?
- Who is supervising (department, relative, foster parent, etc.)?
- Who is transporting?
- Who is the visit with?
- Are both parents visiting together or separate? Is anyone else attending or allowed to attend (such as relatives or family friends)?
- Where are the visits taking place?
- Are there any rules about the location (e.g., does it have to be in a public place)?
- Are there phone or video visits, in addition to in-person?
- Does the call need to be on speakerphone?
- How long should the calls or visits last?
- If the parent isn't there on arrival, how long should the foster parent and child wait before leaving?
- Is the parent required to confirm the visit the day before or the day of?

Set up accounts.

Some foster parents wish to keep parent contact separate with different email and phone accounts. You can use Google Voice or a separate phone, along with a new email address for communication and video calls with parents. Do this early so it's all ready to go when contact and visits begin. Make sure the worker has this information to pass along to parents.

Align on what to bring.

Some workers do not want foster parents to bring anything to visits, and they want the parent(s) to show they can handle all of their child's needs. Other times, the foster parent is asked to bring some or all supplies for the visit (below is a checklist). It may give the parent(s) the wrong impression if you bring all of the child's needed items, so it can be helpful for everyone to get on the same page about who is bringing what.

Bring a communication journal.

If you don't have direct contact or your contact is limited, you can communicate updates and questions with parents through a communication journal. Even if the parent isn't responding, consider continuing to provide updates. At some point, the parent(s) may respond, and you want to make sure the journal is there when they are ready or need it.

Information you can include in the journal:

- Activities:
    - » What they did last weekend
    - » New movies they watched
    - » New food they tried
    - » New milestone
    - » What's going on at school
    - » Trying a new sport or hobby

    - Crafts or art projects
    - Funny things they said (little moments matter too)
- Upcoming:
    - Appointments the parent(s) may need or want to be at (including soccer games, dance recitals, doctor's appointments, etc.). Check with the worker first to make sure the parents are allowed to be there
    - Important dates for the child (big test, first day of school, starting camp, etc.)
    - Photos
    - Questions for the parent(s)
    - Words of encouragement—judge this based on your relationship and make sure it's from the heart. Simple kindness can be meaningful too. "I hope you have a great week," or "Logan told me that you make the best lasagna. Sounds delicious!"

Have a Plan B.

Even if visits are confirmed by the parent(s), sometimes things happen and the parents are a no-show. It's good to have a backup plan (like visiting a park) that is consistent each visit day in case the visit doesn't happen.

If their parent consistently doesn't show up at visits, you can ask the worker if it makes sense to get confirmation once the parent arrives at the visit facility before you leave your home with the children. For younger kids, who might not remember there was supposed to be a visit, if the parent doesn't confirm it, you may choose not to mention it, so the child isn't reminded and then let down.

Don't assume elevated behaviors mean they don't want to visit.

This is a common misconception I see from new foster parents, and I also was confused about this when I first started. While some younger kids may be scared or hesitant to visit their parent(s), in many cases, seeing their parent(s) and then leaving them again can be incredibly sad and difficult for kids to experience over and over again. You may notice more heightened emotions or dysregulation after the visit. It may look like they didn't enjoy the visit, when in reality, they are dealing with the mixed emotions of connecting with their parent(s) and then being separated again.

What to Bring to an In-Person Visit

Below is a list of things you may want to bring to a visit. Just a reminder: Not all items may be needed or appropriate. Workers may want the parent(s) to be responsible for some of these items and/or the parent(s) may want to take ownership of them.

For a daytime visit:

- ☐ Communication journal and pen
- ☐ Medical equipment or medication labeled with child's name and instructions
- ☐ Comfort item/transition item that the child brings from the foster home to the visit and then back to the foster home
- ☐ Items to share such as photos, the kid's artwork, completed schoolwork, etc.
- ☐ Homework/school projects for school-age youth, so parents can help them with their schoolwork, and to help make sure they don't get behind at school

- ☐ Baby-feeding supplies
- ☐ Diaper bag including plenty of diapers and wipes, trash bag for dirty clothes/diapers, hand sanitizer, change of clothing, and changing pad
- ☐ Water bottle/snacks/meals—if the parent is experiencing food insecurity, you can consider bringing extra drinks and snacks so that everyone can share
- ☐ Toys/books/sensory items because the visit location may have very little for the children to do during the visit
- ☐ Car kit such as a change of clothing, cold drink, and emotional-support items for the child for after the visit (these items stay in the car in case they are needed)

For overnight visits, consider all items in the above list to see if it makes sense to pack them for an overnight. You may need to add nighttime supports and toiletries. If overnight visits are leading up to reunification, you can pack things that will *stay* at their parent's house (such as a bin of toys, clothing, or shoes). This helps the move happen gradually over a few weeks.

Visit Nuances by Type

Phone calls:

- Before the call, understand the monitoring requirements. For example, can the youth talk in their room with their door shut? Do you need to be able to hear the conversation? Explain the rules to the youth ahead of time so they aren't surprised during the call. Also remind the parent(s) if you are listening to the conversation at the beginning. 💬 "I'm required to monitor the call, so it'll be on speaker."

- Some kids do best with a warning that the call will be happening soon. You can help them brainstorm things that they may want to share with their parent(s), such as what they had for lunch, what they did at school, or what they are playing with right now.
- For babies, phone calls can be tough, because sometimes babies are completely silent. You can offer simple narration for the parent(s). 💬 "Norah is smiling and listening to you." "Norah is starting to close her eyes to go to sleep."
- Younger children may not have the skills for managing a phone call or sustaining a conversation. Foster parents may have to facilitate. Consider having the call during snack time or a seated activity.
- Older youth may be more independent with the calls. If there are some tricky moments in the conversations, you can figure out a hand signal the youth can use if they want to change subjects or end the call. You can step in to help change the topic or wrap up the conversation, if the youth would like your help. If you end the call early, make sure you let the worker know and provide the reason.

Video calls:

- For babies, you can start the first few minutes with a quick update on the baby, and then share with the parent(s) that you'll put the phone on a stand pointed them. While silence can be a little uncomfortable, it is okay! This is their time with their baby, and parents can spend that time how they wish. If you'd like, you can put on soft lullaby music in the background.
- You can engage babies and little ones with a toy or play mat. You can

also offer to feed them during the call so the parent(s) can watch and talk to them while they drink a bottle.

- For younger children, try to set up a video space in a playroom or at the table, where the camera can be positioned and stay for the entirety of the visit. This helps you avoid running around your home with your camera with the child. For the video space, include a snack, a drink, engaging toys, or a craft activity.
- If the parent(s) or youth would like assistance with how to spend the time together on video, you can suggest things like:
  - » Reading a book together
  - » Playing show-and-tell
  - » Playing a two-player mobile or web-based game
  - » Making up games like "Can you find something yellow to show Daddy?" Go through all of the colors of the rainbow.
  - » Playing Twenty Questions
  - » Playing Battleship (give the parent(s) a board and pieces to keep at their house)
  - » Preparing a meal and/or eat together
  - » Having the youth practice/play their instrument for their parent(s)

In person:

- If the baby soils their diaper on the way to the visit, change them before the visit begins.
- Offer to keep the stroller and/or baby carrier at the visit location for the parent(s) to use. If the parent is pumping breast milk for their baby (with worker permission), ask to use the facility's fridge to store the milk, and bring a cooler for the ride home.

- If the child is potty training, bring related items such as a travel potty seat or extra cleanup supplies if an accident occurs.
- Try to keep the routine around visits as consistent as possible. This can be supportive for all ages: Use the same verbal and body language when foreshadowing, pack the same types of items each time, and plan for a consistent post-visit routine.
- Some youth may be uncertain or anxious about how the visits with their parent(s) will go. You can request to take the youth to the visit space ahead of time or to start with shorter visits. If they are very nervous, there may be an opportunity to have their worker or CASA attend the visit with them.
- For tweens and teens, they may want to bring a calming item/activity (such as a book they are reading, a coloring book or teen sticker book, Pokémon cards, or knitting supplies). Be sure to label anything they bring and avoid bringing a precious/irreplaceable item.
- If little ones struggle to engage at the beginning of the visit, give them a fun task to do upon arrival. 💬 "Here are the new bubbles. You can hold these and bring them to your dad once we get there!" And if younger kids struggle leaving their parent(s) at the end, try to collaborate with the parent(s) on a plan for them to give a warning before the visit is over, or you can join for the last five minutes of playtime to help ease this transition. The parent's support can go a long way in helping the child transition. You can call a team meeting with the parent(s) to brainstorm ideas.
- For babies and little ones, it may be helpful to set up a lovey or stuffed animal exchange system so that you can take home a comfort item that smells like their parent(s) at each visit. This can help with the transitions.

- Before you leave, ask when the baby was fed, had a diaper change, and if they napped during the visit so you know what they may need when you get home.

Overnights:

- Send a lovey that smells like you to help provide comfort while the child is away.
- Write down the sleep and feeding schedule for the parent(s) to help maintain consistency.
- Use visual storytelling or toys to explain that they will spend the night with their parent and then return to your house.
- For babies and little ones, ease them back into your home with care and connection, such as rocking, reading a book, baby massage, or a warm bath. For older kids, you can connect through a walk around the block, building LEGO sets together, sharing a meal from their favorite restaurant, or watching a show together.
- Leave an encouraging or "thinking of you" note in their suitcase with their items.
- When they return, you may want to avoid scheduling intense activities (like a big outing) or "boring" activities like running errands or chores.

Strategies for Unique Situations

Candy and soda are a given at visits.

Generally speaking, unless there is a medical or safety concern, parents have the right to feed their children however they wish at visits. Consider a stop at the park on the way home to burn off energy or requesting caffeine-free drinks be given if the visit happens in the evening. If there are more significant concerns, get a note with dietary needs from the child's pediatrician, dentist, or dietitian.

Kids Not Wanting to Go to the Visit

Below are some additional things you can do to help with this transition.

- Talk to the youth about why they don't want to go. You may find that it's something that can be fixed or changed to make it a better experience for them.
- Take note of your own demeanor/facial expressions when talking about the visit. Kids will look to you for how to feel about a new situation.
- Remind them who will be there: parents, siblings, relatives, worker, family friend, etc.
- If you foster with a partner, try changing up who takes them to the visit and see if they are more open to going with your partner.
- Be mindful of the timing of the visit and what the kids are doing right before the visit. For example, transitioning from a TV show or playing at a park to getting into the car for a visit may be extra challenging because kids might not want to stop the current activity.
- Pack an activity that the child is excited to do. Get their help with packing the bag.
- Stay for a few minutes at the beginning to ease the transition.
- Get help from the department transporting the child to the visit.
- Ask for the monitor or parent(s) to give the child a five-minute warning before the visit will be over.

- Call a team meeting to get more ideas and support from the worker or therapist

Gift-Related Concerns

One way that parents show their love and care for their children is to provide gifts for them at the visits. It can cause some jealousy or sharing concerns with other children in your home. Children can become very protective of items that have been given to them by their parent(s). Collaborate with all of the kids in the home to come up with a plan for special toys, and how sharing and storing them will work.

Another thing that sometimes comes up for foster parents is running out of room in their home to store toys and gifts, especially if the parents bring large items for their child. It's okay to have an honest conversation with the parent(s) about your space constraints. Start from a place of gratitude, and collaborate on a solution. For example, perhaps toys are brought and played with at the visit but stored at the parent's home. Or you can do a toy rotation with the parent(s) and bring older toys for them to store in their home for their children.

Additionally, sometimes parents do not treat siblings equally, or gifts that are given are dangerous for children or not age appropriate. It may be a good idea to loop in the worker and see how they suggest you handle this.

Visits with an Incarcerated Parent

Logistics vary, so try your best to get as much information as possible before the visit. For example, what are you allowed to bring, including things that the child might need while they are there? How will contact be set up? For example, are children allowed to hug their parent(s)? Does everything need to be in a clear bag? Can drawings be brought for the parent(s) to keep? Understand that visiting hours are open to others, so you may see other family members or their parent's friends during this time too.

When it comes to visits, there's a lot of behind-the-scenes work that's done by foster parents. It can feel exhausting managing it all. I found that once you get into a rhythm with visits, they go much more smoothly for everyone involved. Be sure you are getting time to decompress too. Most people don't realize how draining this part of fostering can be. It isn't seen, but it's felt.

19
Advocating for and Setting Up Services

TL;DR: Advocating in a system that is broken beyond repair requires foster parents to be ultra detailed and organized, be a squeaky wheel, leverage the entire team, and persevere through roadblocks.

Advocating in Multiple Systems as a Foster Parent

Parents can be their kids' biggest cheerleaders and advocates. They show up to appointments and conferences, and ask questions, get second opinions, research topics, and beyond. Parents are there to make sure their child is being treated properly by peers and adults, and that they have access to the accommodations they need. Foster parents do this too in similar spaces, like at the doctor or at school. Additionally, foster parents advocate within multiple systems that are filled with red tape, policies, and roadblocks. This includes child welfare, family court, department of mental health, early intervention services, disability services, healthcare/Medicaid, and special education, including therapeutic schools.

If you've arrived at this chapter, you may be witnessing firsthand the cracks in the system and you may be worried that the child in your care is getting missed. In my years of advocating, I have come to realize that it's a marathon, not a sprint. The system is designed to only work for people who can be a squeaky wheel and have the capacity to not give up. It's frustrating and exhausting, but I can tell you, when you finally succeed in your advocacy efforts, it is worth it.

Advocacy Basics from the Community

Know the policies, rules, and laws governing your county.

If you aren't sure, ask the worker where you can find the written directives. If they are telling you it's a rule, then they should be able to send you documentation about the rule to learn more. 💬 "Can you please show me where I can find more about this rule? This isn't something that was covered in my preservice training, and I want to understand the full context."

- **Be one of the experts in the room.** People will give your opinions and ideas more weight if you show that you understand what's going on and are on top of the details regarding the child. Even though you are a first-time foster parent, you are the *only* person with the child consistently, each and every day. Come prepared with paperwork and documents readily available. Plan ahead what you will share about the youth's strengths and needs, and what questions you will ask. If you have your own area of professional expertise (like if you are a teacher or doctor), you can include this information as it pertains to the conversation.
- **Be a good recordkeeper.** Keeping track of when you spoke with people and when things were promised, *in writing*, will serve you and the child in the future when you are advocating. When someone says that they will work on something for you, ask them for a

general idea of when you can expect to hear back. This doesn't have to be rude or pushy, but it can help align everyone on the next step. 💬 "Thanks for working on that referral. Any sense as to when you think I'll hear from them? What's typical?" If they say, "I'm not sure," or "It ranges," you can offer a guess and let them give a simple yes or no. 💬 "In the past it's taken about a month. Does that sound right?" or "I am new to this—so would it be like two weeks or two months?"

- **When reporting concerns or an incident, use facts and observations, not opinions.** There's a time and place for your opinions, but when dealing with sensitive situations, you may get a better response from workers or attorneys if you state what you *know*, not what you *think*. 💬 "The parent(s) arrived thirty minutes late, had slurred speech, and dozed off during playtime. They also stumbled three times while playing outside with their child," rather than ✖ "I think the parent(s) came to the visit drunk and doesn't care about being sober for their child."
- **Humanize the request and remain child centered.** It may seem obvious, but when you use the word "child" or their name, things feel more personal and important. Also, focus the request on the child's needs, rather than your needs. 💬 "Taylor is only eight and has so much potential. He's two grade levels behind and could really use someone in his corner who understands the educational system. Are you able to look into a CASA or a specialized educational advocate to help get services lined up for him at school?" might be more effective than ✖ "I am overwhelmed and need help from an attorney because I'm not getting anywhere with the school on my own."

- **Empower the youth to use their voice.** Your advocacy efforts are meaningful, but don't forget to let youth speak for themselves too. Foster parents can be incredible teachers of how to self-advocate by preparing youth for meetings and letting them answer questions first. The kid can use their voice to inform a worker about what's going on, talk directly to their therapist about what they experienced, ask their attorney for something they need, explain to their psychiatrist what it feels like to be on the medications, or tell the judge directly what it's like to be in foster care.

Roadblocks and Red Tape

All of the rules and policies can make it difficult to find your way through the systems that feed into child welfare. Some common ones you may run into:

PROBLEM

Slow response/delays in approval/multistep approvals (requires workers, supervisors, judges, and/or parents to approve)

STRATEGIES

Ask early. Copy supervisors on requests. Include dates or deadlines, if applicable. Focus on the child's best interests, rather than your convenience or needs. Use other team members as advocates in addition to you, to possibly speed things up or to get attention from the worker (e.g., submit a letter from their doctor).

PROBLEM

Incomplete or missing paperwork

STRATEGIES

Try multiple sources of information, such as the pediatrician, pharmacist, or school administrators, in addition to the worker.

PROBLEM

The child is severely behind academically, and the IEP assessment period is taking longer than it's supposed to.

STRATEGIES

Ask for accommodations and supports *now*. It doesn't hurt to start talking with their teacher(s) about how to help them get caught up. Call a meeting with admin and the foster care liaisons for the district to request accommodations. Get the child's advocate involved to speak directly with the school. Request additional funding for outside tutoring services or educational therapy. Find a local education-related nonprofit to fill gaps while you wait.

PROBLEM

Stipend is delayed or inaccurate.

STRATEGIES

Confirm the department or agency has your correct address. Fill out direct deposit forms to avoid mail delays. Call the level-of-care office or department directly, and request a level-of-care assessment. Call the foster parent helpline. Discuss the issue with the child's advocate. In the meantime, seek other funding sources through WIC, childcare reimbursement programs, foster closets, or free school lunch programs.

YOUR EFFORTS ARE MEANINGFUL AND SEEN, AS NOTED BY THIS COMMUNITY MEMBER

"I work in the foster care world, and what I value the most is the foster parents who always show up and advocate."

Working with Advocates and Going to Court

Advocates

When I mention the child's advocate, I'm referring to their attorney, CASA (court-appointed special advocate), or GAL (guardian ad litem). Across the United States, it is incredible how dramatically different representation is for youth in foster care. Some youth have an attorney who checks in regularly, while others have little to no legal support. As someone who grew up in a family of attorneys, I see the incredible value of youth having their *own* representation in court.

Attorneys and GALs often have large caseloads, so it can be helpful to ask them how to get in contact with them if there's an emergency or urgent matter. They may want you to put something specific in the subject line of an email, call their direct cell phone, or get in touch with their supervisor.

Your time with the advocate may be limited. At times, I've only had a few moments to talk as I walk with them toward the courtroom. Be prepared to share the most important thing you need to communicate. They may simply ask you, "Does the child need anything right now?" or "Are there any concerns?" so be prepared to respond in a simple, straightforward way.

If the child doesn't have an advocate in their life, the foster parent can step in to help. In many places, foster youth have written rights or a bill of rights. Familiarize yourself with their rights and review them with the youth. Reference these rights when advocating.

Court

You can also familiarize yourself with the county's family court policies. You can look this up online, ask the child's advocate (if they have one), call the courthouse, or ask in local online foster parent groups. These policies and procedures vary and may cover things like:

- What information foster parents can and can't receive regarding court and case plans (remember, confidentiality is important!).
- If foster parents are allowed to attend court, and if so, for the entirety or just for part of the hearing.

- What documents foster parents can submit to court, such as a caregiver form, statement, photos, etc.

If you can attend court, you may hear updates as to how the case is progressing and possibly about when reunification or a transition will occur. This can be helpful for you so you can start to prepare your heart. The judge may also call upon you to speak or share an update. Whenever we had court, I would prepare a statement just in case I was called on.

When you attend court, you may also have a chance to meet with the child's advocate ahead of the hearing. If you plan to go, consider emailing the advocate to let them know you want to talk to them so they can check in with you before the hearing.

Setting Up Services

"Services" usually refers to professional help for the youth. This could be mental health therapy, in-home behavioral support, developmental therapies, academic support, and beyond.

Often an assessment occurs to determine the need, a referral is made, and then there is sometimes a waitlist. There may also be a delay because parents or judges have to sign off on specific assessments or services. It can be challenging and frustrating when things do not begin quickly enough for the child. Some strategies you could try:

- **Use at-home diagnostic tools** as a starting point (such as Ages and Stages Questionnaires (ASQ) or the CDC Milestone Tracker app). Take these results to the worker and/or pediatrician. Remember, trauma responses may look like other disabilities or disorders, and often these at-home diagnostic tools don't take trauma into account. View these as an important beginning to your advocacy for support but know that a professional will need to assess the child, and their trauma background will need to be considered.

- **Check if you can self-refer.** Depending on the service, and where you live, foster parents may be able to request services directly and don't need a special referral. You still likely will need worker and/or parent approval for some services.
- **Call and check to make sure they are still on the waitlist and get an idea of how long it will take.** You want to make sure that all of your information is correct. You can continue to call periodically (like monthly) to get an update.
- **Call other agencies.** If you are on the waitlist at one agency, you may be able to call around to other agencies to see if they have availability. You may also see if the pediatrician can submit a referral to a different service provider. It's okay to be on more than one waitlist.
- **Seek out alternatives while you wait.** For example, you can check with local nonprofits to see if they have an offering that could be helpful (such as peer support groups or gatherings). The school district may be able to provide counseling, peer or friendship groups, or specialized groups (like grief groups). These may be helpful while you wait for therapy to begin.
- **Support them at home.** Research the child's specific need/diagnosis, or take specialized trainings on the topic to find ways to better support at home while you wait. You may also find parent groups on Facebook or Reddit that can refer you to trainings or help you come up with ideas of things that might help the youth.

Still struggling?

If you feel that the child or the case is being *severely underserved*, or perhaps someone on the team is being unethical or doing things that go against county policies, you may need to escalate these concerns even more.

- Some foster parents have had success writing a letter to the judge explaining what is going on or needed.
- You can consider calling your local CASA office, and explain what's happening and see if you can self-refer (or get part of the process started).
- In some places you can call a foster parent helpline to report issues.
- Other foster parents in your county may also have a contact for someone higher up in the department that they can share with you. It doesn't hurt to ask!
- You can file a formal grievance with the department.
- You may want to change agencies after the youth leaves your home. Be careful changing agencies if you still have a child in your home. Often the child is the responsibility of the agency, and they may move the child out of your home if you change to a different agency.

With all of these things, it's important to note that when you are more direct and stronger in your advocacy, *you might face retaliation*. It's an advocacy balancing act. Push, then pause and reflect. Push, then pause and reflect. You want to be loud so the youth gets help, but you also don't want to be seen as too difficult, resulting in the worker removing the child or claiming you are being aggressive or inappropriate. Make sure you've maintained professionalism, exhausted all efforts, and given sufficient time for people to get back to you.

Take Care.

There is so much to think about and process as a foster parent. I know it often feels like no one really understands all the day-to-day, in-the-moment work you are doing, but please know it is meaningful and it is noticed.

I want to close this book with some words of encouragement. I hope this inspires you to keep going during the hard seasons. You are making a difference.

THANK YOU FOR BEING THERE TO HELP.

"The index card [my foster mom] wrote down on day one with a list of favorite things and allergies was nice. She had one for every kid she raised. It was a small gesture, but that list of favorites was referenced for birthdays and holidays. That index card was one of the first indications that I was home for as long as I lived there."

"My now adoptive mom told me a million times, 'It's not your fault.' I needed to hear that on repeat for years. She also baked me a birthday cake, which was the first time anyone had ever done that. My now adoptive dad introduced me to everyone he met as his daughter even before I was legally adopted. It probably made him seem like he had a child [when he was] in high school, but he didn't care what people would think. I really appreciated that. He also played basketball with me for hours and never kept score. He came to all my recitals and told me he was proud of me."

"My foster mom showed me that she was happy with herself and with her life. Seeing her happy told me: 'Oh, maybe things really are okay here.'"

"Being a teen is hard. Being in foster care is harder, but at least I always had a caregiver that showed up every single day, even when they didn't feel good or were upset with me."

"At the end of the day, you are doing your best to keep these kiddos safe. It's exhausting trying to keep up with appointments, meetings, home visits, parent visits, work, school, daycare but you are doing so much good for these kids and their families. You are making an impact. You are stronger than you think you are and will make it to the end of the day!"

"It's the foster parents who show up with a surreal kind of patience, know when to get help (and are willing to get help), and never fail to advocate for the kids' needs that make such a difference. It's when they show flexibility to adjust to a new parenting style, try different techniques, and show an unwavering commitment to being there for that child."

I signed up
to change a *life*...

...but I realized it was *my life*
that was changing.

Glossary

When I first started fostering, it felt like I was learning a whole new language. Let me get you up to speed.

Important note: Individual counties and states use these terms and acronyms differently. The list below is crowdsourced, so the way your worker uses these terms may vary slightly. Never feel embarrassed about asking for clarification!

Foster Care Programs

Emergency foster care: Usually emergency foster care providers are foster parents that are willing to take kids who have just been removed from their parent(s), during all hours of the day (nights, weekends, and holidays). In some places, kids in emergency homes only stay for a short amount of time until a longer-term home is identified. Each county handles emergency placements differently, so check with a worker.

Medical foster home: This typically refers to a foster home that provides specialized care for children who have medical needs that require daily support (also known as medically fragile youth). Often a nurse is added to the child's professional team. Some counties will require at least one foster parent to be a medical professional, but in other places, a foster parent can be trained to provide the necessary medical care to the youth. These foster parents typically are required to receive additional training, and they receive a higher stipend each month for the day-to-day needs of the youth.

Respite provider: Respite care is provided by an approved caregiver with whom a child stays with when their foster parents cannot be present. It's typically overnight care for several days, but in some places, you can get respite for just a few hours. Respite is often paid for by the county and there's no additional cost for the foster parent.

Therapeutic or treatment foster care (TFC) or enhanced foster care (EFC): This often refers to foster homes who care for youth with a higher level of behavioral and emotional support needs. Sometimes youth with medical needs are also placed in a treatment foster home. These foster parents typically are required to receive additional training, and they receive a higher stipend each month for the day-to-day needs of the youth.

Common Terms and Acronyms

504 Plan: A plan for providing accommodations that allow the child to participate fully in school based on their needs, as required by Section 504 of the Rehabilitation Act of 1973.

Absent without leave (AWOL): When a youth leaves your home or "runs away."

Adoption Assistance Program (AAP): After a child is adopted from foster care, they may qualify for financial or medical benefits. Check with the adoption worker about what program exists in your county or state.

Advocates: Someone who is representing the child in court or advocates on their behalf in other settings. This can include an Attorney Ad Litem (AAL), Guardian Ad Litem (GAL), or Court-Appointed Special Advocate (CASA).

Child and Family Team Meetings (CFTM): These meetings are when the entire team gets together to discuss needs or updates on the case. They can also be referred to as a Family Involvement Meeting (FIM) or Family Team Meeting (FTM).

Child Welfare/Foster Care Departments and Agencies: These are the agencies and departments that manage the foster care system in your area. Each county and state will use different terminology for these programs. These are some of the common acronyms used:

» **CPA (child-placing agent or agency)**
» **CPS (Child Protective Services)**

- » DCF (Department of Children and Families)
- » DCFS (Department of Children and Family Services)
- » DCS (Department of Child Service)
- » DHHS (Department of Health and Human Services)
- » DHS (Department of Human Services)
- » DSS (Department of Social Services)
- » FFA (foster family agency)
- » RFA (resource family agency)

Child Welfare Professionals: Case managers (CM) or case workers (CW) are child welfare professionals who work directly with kids and families and oversee the foster care case. They also may train and support foster families. There are also AWs (adoption workers), who are workers who specialize in finalizing the adoption of a youth in foster care or support postadoption. In some places, the person who is managing the foster care case is a social worker (SW).

Commercial sexual exploitation of children (CSEC): This is a form of child sexual abuse, sometimes referred to as "trafficking." There are often specialized departments or workers that support and interventions in these cases.

Disruption: When the child placement ends earlier than planned and a new home or facility has to be established for the child. Disruptions often occur due to safety concerns for the child.

Extended foster care (EFC): Foster care programs that extend past the age of eighteen.

Family and Medical Leave Act (FMLA): This allows employees to take unpaid time off work without worrying about losing their jobs. Foster families are included in this act, but depending on your employment type and business specifics, you may or may not qualify. Check with HR!

Former foster youth (FFY): Typically refers to someone who spent any amount of time in foster care.

Group Homes: A type of out-of-home placement where many kids live in one home or facility that's supervised by staff.

Indian Child Welfare Act (ICWA): Federal law that governs the removal and placement of children who are Indigenous.

Individualized Education Program (IEP): Legal document outlining special education services.

Intensive outpatient program (IOP): This is usually a program for kids who require intensive support but are able to safely remain in their foster home. This is often multiple hours a day and/or multiple days a week.

Interstate Compact on the Placement of Children (ICPC): A contract across states that outlines how kids in foster care are placed across state lines.

Level of care (LOC): This identifies the type of care the child needs.

Many child welfare departments use LOC to determine services and monthly stipend.

Lifebook: Lifebooks can take many forms, depending on the child and their life experiences. For foster parents, a lifebook is often a physical, personalized photo album or scrapbook documenting the child's time in foster care. The goal of a life book is often to preserve memories of their time in foster care and the connections they made. This book remains with the youth after they leave the foster home.

Nonrelated extended family member (NREFM): An adult that has a meaningful relationship with a child but is not biologically related.

Postadoption contact agreement (PACA): An agreement to allow for birth family contact after an adoption.

Professional team: A multidisciplinary team of people who work together to support the child and make decisions about their care. This can include child welfare worker, mental health therapist, developmental therapist(s), behaviorist, advocate, teachers, and other professionals.

Residential treatment center (RTC): This is a place for full-time care of a child who requires a high level of care to keep themselves or others safe. You can usually visit the youth while they are there—please ask!

Reunification: When a child returns to their parent(s) after being in out-of-home care (such as foster care, kinship care, or group home).

Secondary trauma: This occurs when someone is deeply affected by another person's traumatic experiences, even though they didn't experience it firsthand.

Termination of parental rights (TPR): When this happens, the parent loses all legal parental authority over the child.

Appendix

Parenting

- *The Whole-Brain Child* by Daniel J. Siegel, MD, and Tina Payne Bryson
- *Raising Kids with Big Baffling Behaviors* by Robyn Gobbel
- The How To Talk series by Adele Faber and Elaine Mazlish
- *The A–Z of Therapeutic Parenting* by Sarah Naish
- *The Explosive Child* by Ross W. Greene, PhD
- *Parent Yourself First* by Bryana Kappadakunnel
- Bryan Post training series (books, website, and YouTube channel)

Feeding Related

- Growing Intuitive Eating Course on YouTube from Dr. Taylor Arnold (this is a free course)
- *Love Me, Feed Me*, by Katja Rowell, MD.

Crisis Hotlines/Text Lines and Support

- 988 Suicide and Crisis Lifeline: 988lifeline.org

- The Childhelp National Child Abuse Hotline: ChildHelpHotline.org
- The Trevor Project LGBTQ+ crisis services: thetrevorproject.org/crisis-services/
- The National Runaway Safeline: 1800Runaway.org
- National Domestic Violence Hotline: TheHotline.org
- National Sexual Assault Hotline: RAINN.org
- National Sexual Violence Resource Center: nsvrc.org

Online Training Opportunities

- National Foster Parent Association Training Institute: nfpati.org
- FosterParentCollege.com
- FosterClub.com
- American Red Cross (first aid, CPR, water safety, etc.): redcross.org

Acknowledgments

Creating and sharing about foster care has been one of the greatest privileges of my life. This book wouldn't exist if it wasn't for the millions of people who watched, considered, and chimed in with their own stories of hope, courage, and care. You remind me each and every day that small acts of showing up are what spark progress, change, and healing. Thank you for showing up in your homes, communities, and online to help.

Jaymi Lynn, thank you for combing through the details of this book with care and compassion. Your dedication to improving the circumstances of people impacted by foster care is extraordinary. You are a gift, and anyone who has a chance to learn from you is changed for the better. Thank you for your expertise and insights. Your heart and wisdom are echoed in every chapter of this book.

To Dr. Taylor Arnold and Dr. Melissa Jinariu, thank you for lending your expertise and adding depth and impact.

Thank you to all of my early readers for being so generous with your time and honesty. It elevated this guidebook to new heights.

To the kids who've called me Mom, Laura, Nana, Lala, and "that girl." I thought about you as I wrote each page of this book. Thank you for teaching me what it means to be brave, resilient, and to love with your full heart.

And thank you to my husband, Chris, who has been my partner in every part of my life since the day we met. You filled a hole in my heart, which allowed me to pursue a life I could not have imagined for myself. You've traveled across the world to support me while I reached career goals I never thought were possible. Fostering with you was a journey of a lifetime. I look back on those experiences and am grateful that you were there. I couldn't have done it without you. Thank you for staying up late to read (and reread and then reread again) this book. I literally could not have written this book without you. I love you!

Index

B

G

H

N

O

P

R

S

T

V

W

About the Author

Photo © Richard Giorman

Laura is a content creator and mentor who draws from her experiences as a therapeutic foster parent, as well as shared stories and feedback from the community she's built. She supports and empowers new foster parents through getting licensed and fostering for the first time. With practical tips, trauma-conscious considerations, and relatable stories, Laura helps others approach the complexities of foster care. Her mission is to raise awareness, advocate for children in care, and inspire foster parents to feel confident and prepared in their journey.